BEYOND HALLUCINATIONS

HOW THE VALUE OF AI TRANSCENDS ITS FLAWS

MARSHALL S. MARTINEAU

EARNSHAW BOOKS

Beyond Hallucinations
By Marshall S. Martineau

Trade Paper: 978-988-8904-90-7
Digital: 978-988-8904-89-1

COMPUTERS / ARTIFICIAL INTELLIGENCE / GENERAL

EB261

Published in Hong Kong by Earnshaw Books Ltd.

Contents

Preface

Why This Book, Why Now?

Let's be honest, you've probably used an AI tool at some point and been disappointed. Maybe you asked it for a historical fact and it confidently gave you nonsense, or perhaps you asked it to write a simple email and it produced something so generic it was basically useless. You're not alone. The story of AI for most people is a story of incredible promises followed by—at times—underwhelming, and sometimes downright weird, results.

The word everyone uses to describe these failures is "hallucination." It's a catchy, slightly scary term that's come to define the entire conversation around Artificial Intelligence. And that's a problem, not the least because it reveals a curious double standard. We obsess over AI's flaws while casually accepting that humans make mistakes all the time. Think about it: we get bad advice from friends, hear misremembered facts from colleagues, and see biased news and stories in the media. We call these what they are—mistakes (or worse), not 'hallucinations.' We note them and move on. By branding AI errors with such an alarming label, we hold it to a standard of perfection we don't demand from each other, or even from ourselves.

Focusing only on hallucinations is like reviewing a car based solely on its cup holders. Yes, they are useful, but they aren't even close to reflecting the whole story. By obsessing over the errors, we're missing the bigger picture: a technological shift that is reshaping how we all work, create, and think. The trap is to be so focused on the fear of being wrong that we miss the opportunity to use these amazing tools to, literally, change our lives.

So this isn't a book about hallucinations—it's about what comes after them. The real story of AI begins once we stop treating its mistakes as barriers and start seeing them as growing pains on the way to something extraordinary. Moving beyond the hallucinations means learning to work with imperfection, to experiment, to explore—and to unlock the immense creative and practical potential that sits just on the other side of doubt.

This book was written to change the conversation. It's for the curious and the skeptics—the leaders, creators, and professionals who have heard the hype, played around with the new toy and experienced a letdown, and are now wondering to what extent this thing is reliable. It's a book about moving past disappointment to find the practical, everyday value that's hiding in plain sight —about how you understand, embrace, and manoeuvre through the AI world of today and tomorrow.

Why now? Because the window of opportunity is closing. Not to sound dramatic, but the teams and organizations that first figure out how to work with AI—not just talk about its flaws—are the ones that will build the future. The rest will be left wondering what happened. This is your chance to get ahead of the curve.

A Note on Perspective

I'm not an AI researcher or a Silicon Valley coder, I'm a pragmatic businessman. Over the last 30 years I've worked across multiple countries and cultures, helping individuals and organizations solve real-world problems. I look at AI not as a magical black box, but as a tool, a powerful, flawed, and often misunderstood tool.

My perspective, you could say, is that of a translator. I sit between the world of frontier models and the world of quarterly reports, marketing deadlines, and team meetings. I'm less interested in how the technology works and more interested in what it can do for you. How can it make your team more creative?

How can it help you find useful signals amidst the noise of your data? How can it free up a few or many hours in your week?

You won't find dense academic theory here. Instead, you'll find practical frameworks, real-world examples, and a healthy dose of realism. I believe in being up-front about the limitations of AI while remaining fiercely optimistic about its potential. It's not about hype; it's about help.

How to Read This Book

Think of this book as a journey in five parts. You can read it cover to cover, or you can jump to the sections that matter most to you right now. I've added a summary at the beginning of each chapter so you can quickly decide if this is one you want to explore. You certainly don't need to do a deep dive into every chapter of this book, but if you do, I can promise you a thought-provoking journey through the ideas, innovations, and contradictions shaping this new age of AI.

> **Part I: Understanding now the Hallucination Narrative lays the groundwork.**
> We'll tackle the term "hallucination" head-on, explore why it dominates the discussion, and look at the psychology of why first impressions of technology are so hard to shake and introduce a new field guide to AI errors to distinguish between different ways AI can be 'wrong'.
>
> **Part II: Beyond the Hallucinations is where we get practical.**
> This is the "how-to" section, focused on what AI actually gets right and the specific workflows you can use to make it reliable. We'll cover everything from

designing reliable prompts and evaluation techniques for non-engineers to the role of synthetic data.

Part III: The Human Side explores the most important part of the equation: us.
How do we learn to trust (but verify)? What does it take to build a culture of responsible AI use that accounts for ethics beyond simple errors? And how does this technology look from different cultural perspectives around the globe?

Part IV: The AI Ecosystem zooms out from the individual user to the global stage.
We'll investigate the powerful forces shaping the entire field: the geopolitics of computer chips, the economics of who pays for intelligence, the pressing legal questions of copyright and accountability, and the critical debate between open and closed AI models.

Part V: Looking Forward explores what's next for both the technology and for you.
We'll discuss how AI is evolving from a simple tool into a true collaborative partner, examine the future of skepticism and how to engage with it, and provide a simple playbook for you to start experimenting with confidence.

So, are you ready to move beyond the hallucinations? Great. Let's get started.

PART 1

UNDERSTANDING THE HALLUCINATION NARRATIVE

1

So, What is a Hallucination Anyway?

If you ask a person for directions in a city they don't know, they'll likely do one of two things. They'll either say, "I'm sorry, I have no idea," or they'll try to help, pointing vaguely in a direction they think is right, filling in the gaps with well-intentioned guesswork. They're not lying; they're just trying to be helpful, and their brain is wired to create a coherent story even when it lacks all the facts. Now, what if a machine does the same thing? We call it a "hallucination" and act shocked, as if a toaster just offered us financial advice.

This chapter is about that word. We're going to break down where it came from, why it stuck, and why it's one of the most misleading and unhelpful metaphors in technology today. More importantly, we're going to explore what's really happening when an AI gets something wrong, and how that compares to the countless errors, biases, and fabrications that we humans produce—and tolerate—every single day. Before we can move past the hallucination narrative, we have to understand it.

The Origins of the Term

The term "hallucination" wasn't born in a marketing meeting. It came from the AI researchers themselves. In the early days of large language models (LLMs), engineers needed a word to describe the phenomenon of a model generating text that was nonsensical, factually incorrect, or untethered from the input it was given. So they borrowed the term from neuroscience, where a hallucination is a perception in the absence of external stimulus. It seemed to fit. The AI was "seeing" things that weren't there, inventing facts and sources with startling confidence. It was a useful piece of technical shorthand for one engineer to describe a specific type of output to another.

The problem started when the term escaped the lab.

Why the Narrative Stuck

For the media and the public, "hallucination" was a gift. It's a word loaded with meaning. It sounds human, psychological, and a little bit dangerous. It conjures images of madness and delusion, of a machine losing its grip on reality. It's a far more compelling story than "stochastic parrot producing a statistically improbable but syntactically coherent token sequence." The narrative stuck for three key reasons:

1. **It's Familiar:** It anchors a complex, alien technology in a human concept we can all understand. We know what it means for a person to hallucinate, so we feel like we know what it means for an AI to do it.
2. **It's Dramatic:** It feeds into our deepest anxieties about artificial intelligence – the fear of machines we can't control, that operate on a logic we can't comprehend. "AI Makes a Factual Error" is a boring headline. "AI Is Hallucinating" is a Hollywood movie plot.
3. **It Confirms Our Bias:** For anyone skeptical of AI, the idea of hallucinations confirms what they already believe: that this technology is unreliable, untrustworthy, and fundamentally broken. It's an easy reason to dismiss it without having to engage with it more deeply.

This perfect storm of familiarity, drama, and confirmation bias is powerful. It's why your boss, your clients, and even your tech-savvy friends are all talking about hallucinations. It has become the central theme in the public's understanding of AI.

The Danger of Stopping at the First Impression

Here's the thing about first impressions: they are incredibly sticky. When we form an initial judgment, our brains actively seek out information that confirms it and filter out information that challenges it. Psychologists call this confirmation bias, and it's why it's so hard to change your mind.

If your first real experience with an LLM was it inventing a fake legal precedent or a non-existent historical figure, that memory becomes a powerful anchor. Every future news story about an AI error reinforces your initial belief. You're trapped. You've seen enough.

But what if that first impression wasn't the whole story? What if it was like judging an entire movie based on the opening scene? In Chapter 4, we'll dive deeper into what I call the "First Try Trap," but for now, just consider this: is it possible that the technology has evolved since your first encounter? Is it possible that the way you were using it wasn't the right way? And is it possible that the errors, while real, are not the most interesting or important part of the story?

Types of Errors: More Than One Way to Be Wrong

When we lump all AI mistakes under the single, scary umbrella of "hallucinations," we lose all nuance. In reality, an AI can be wrong in several different ways, and understanding the differences is key to working with it effectively.

- **Factual Errors**
This is the most straightforward type of mistake. The AI provides a piece of information that is demonstrably false. It might state that the capital of Australia is Sydney (it's Canberra) or that Neil Armstrong walked on the moon in 1968 (it was 1969). These are often caused by the model drawing on incorrect information from its training data.
- **Fabricated Information**
This is a step beyond a simple factual error. Here, the AI invents details, sources, or even entire events. It might cite a research paper that doesn't exist or quote an expert who never said those words. This happens because the model is designed to generate plausible-sounding text, and if it can't find a real source, it will sometimes create one that looks like a real source.
- **Misleading Confidence**
This, in my opinion, is the most dangerous type of error. It's not just that the information is wrong; it's that the AI presents it with the same confident, authoritative tone it uses when the information is correct. There are no verbal tics, no hesitation, no "I think" or "maybe." It delivers falsehoods with the same polish as facts, making it difficult for a non-expert to spot the error.

By breaking down the errors, we move from a vague, fear-based concept—"hallucination"—to a practical, problem-solving mindset. A factual error can be checked. A fabricated source can be identified. And once you're aware of misleading confidence, you learn to treat every output with a healthy dose of professional skepticism—the same skepticism you'd apply to a human consultant, by the way.

Why "Hallucination" Is a Misleading Metaphor

So, why does the metaphor bother me so much? Because it implies the machine has a mind to lose. A hallucination, in humans, is a complex neuro-psychological event. It involves perception, consciousness, and a subjective experience of reality. An LLM has none of those things. It is not conscious. It has no beliefs, no intentions, and no understanding of the world. It is a prediction engine. When you give it a prompt, it is simply calculating the most statistically likely sequence of words to come next, based on the patterns it learned from the vast amount of text it was trained on. An "error" is not a moment of madness; it's a statistical miscalculation. The model has predicted a plausible-sounding sentence that happens to be factually incorrect. That's it. It's a math problem, not a mental health crisis.

Calling it a hallucination anthropomorphizes the machine, giving it a human-like quality it doesn't possess. This does two damaging things:

1. It makes the technology seem spookier and more uncontrollable than it really is.
2. It prevents us from diagnosing the problem correctly and, therefore, from finding the right solutions. You don't fix a math problem with therapy.

Comparing AI Errors with Human Errors

Let's go back to those directions. The helpful but wrong stranger on the street isn't the only way we humans get things wrong. We misremember names. We embellish stories to make them more interesting. We confidently repeat headlines we only skimmed. Our memories are notoriously unreliable, shaped by emotion, suggestion, and the simple passage of time.

If humans misremember, embellish, and sometimes outright

fabricate, why do we expect machines to be flawless storytellers? We hold AI to a standard of perfection that no human could ever meet. A 2012 study found that roughly 50% of people have at least one "impossible" autobiographical memory—a memory of an event that could not possibly have happened. We are, all of us, constantly hallucinating our own pasts. The difference is, we have developed social systems to account for human fallibility. We have fact-checkers in journalism, peer review in science, and the simple wisdom of "getting a second opinion" in daily life. We don't expect any single human to be a perfect source of truth.

Our goal should not be to create an infallible AI—an impossible task—but to develop the same kinds of verification systems and critical thinking skills for our work with machines. The problem isn't that AI makes mistakes. The problem is our expectation that it wouldn't.

The bottom line is this: "hallucination" is a catchy but lazy metaphor. It's a first-impression judgment that has stuck far too long. To truly harness the power of this technology, we need to move beyond the scary stories, understand the different ways it can be wrong, and build the skills to work with it smartly. We need to treat it not as a flawed oracle, but as an incredibly powerful, sometimes-wrong assistant. And as with any assistant, the ultimate responsibility for the work lies with you.

2

A Field Guide to Being 'Wrong'

In Chapter 1, we deconstructed the word "hallucination." We learned it's a catchy but lazy metaphor that lumps all of an AI's failures under one spooky, unhelpful umbrella. By doing that, we miss the point. We treat a machine's statistical miscalculation as a mental health crisis, and because we don't diagnose the problem correctly, we can't find the right fit.

When a chef burns a dish, do you call it a "kitchen hallucination"? No. You call it overcooked. A mechanic doesn't just say a car is "not working." They run a diagnostic and find a specific problem: a clogged fuel filter, a dead battery, a faulty spark plug.

The same is true for AI. Not all errors are the same, and if you want to be a master operator, you need a field guide to AI's various ways of being wrong. This chapter is that guide. We will break down the most common types of AI errors, give each one a clear name, and—most importantly—provide a specific remedy. This moves us from a vague, fear-based reaction to a practical, problem-solving mindset. Let's start with our taxonomy.

1. Fabrication: The Confident Liar

What it is: This is the classic "hallucination" in its purest form. The AI invents a fact, a name, a source, or a date that is demonstrably and completely false. It's not a misunderstanding; it's a creation. This happens because the model's core function is to produce plausible-sounding text, and if it lacks the actual information, it will simply fill in the blanks with something that fits the pattern.

The Signature: Cites a real-sounding but non-existent research paper. Quotes a person who never said those words. Provides a factual claim that you can't verify with a quick search. The output is slick, professional, and entirely made up.

The Remedy: This is where your trust calibration must be set to "low." You can't fix a fabrication with a better prompt. The only remedy is verification. For high-stakes tasks, every single fact, figure, and citation must be checked against a reliable source. For this reason, you should only use AI systems with Retrieval-Augmented Generation (RAG) for factual work, as they are specifically designed to ground their answers in a trusted knowledge base and provide citations for every claim.

2. Misinterpretation: The Bad Listener

What it is: This error isn't about inventing facts; it's about misunderstanding the ones you gave it. The AI misreads your prompt, misinterprets your intent, or gets confused by a nuance in the source text you provided. It has all the right ingredients but puts them together in the wrong order, like a recipe that calls for two cups of flour but you read it as two tablespoons.

The Signature: The AI's response is factually correct but completely misses the point. It gives you a great summary of a document but ignores your specific request to "focus on the financial implications." It writes an excellent email, but the tone is completely wrong for the intended recipient.

The Remedy: The problem here is not the AI's knowledge; it's your briefing. The fix is almost always a better prompt. You must be more clear, more specific, and more directive. The solution is prompt tuning and constraint setting. Re-run the prompt, but this time, add a persona ("Act as a CFO...") and a clear constraint ("Focus exclusively on ROI and budget implications. Do not mention the team's creative process.").

3. Bias: The Unwitting Mirror

What it is: This is one of the most dangerous kinds of errors because it isn't a mistake; it's a reflection. The AI, having been trained on a massive dataset of human language from the internet, learns all of our cultural and historical biases—about gender, race, profession, and nationality. When you ask it to generate content, it will often replicate these biases in subtle but powerful ways.

The Signature: The AI consistently associates certain professions with a single gender ("the engineer and his team," "the nurse and her patient"). Its examples for a high-performing leader are all from a single cultural background. It gives you a hiring recommendation that silently down-ranks qualified candidates from underrepresented groups. The output feels plausible, but a closer look reveals a systemic skew.

The Remedy: The problem here is the training data, not the model's intent. You can't fix a systemic issue with a single prompt. The solution is a combination of data audit and human-in-the-loop oversight. Before you deploy an AI model in a sensitive area like hiring or finance, you must audit the data it was trained on for known biases. Then, you must put human gates in place. For high-stakes decisions, the AI's output should be treated as a draft or a recommendation, never as a final decision. The human expert is the ultimate backstop and the final decision-maker.

4. Omission: The Silent Gap

What it is: This is when the AI fails to include a critical piece of information. It doesn't get something wrong, but it leaves something important out. This often happens because the AI is a "prediction engine," and it simply didn't predict that the omitted information was relevant to your query. The answer it gives you is correct, but it's incomplete, which makes it misleading.

The Signature: The AI summarizes a report and hits all the main points but completely leaves out a critical risk factor that was buried in a footnote. It gives you a list of solutions to a problem, but it neglects to mention the most common and effective one.

The Remedy: This is a classic case of knowing the strengths and weaknesses of your tool. The fix is a retrieval design and human verification. If you're using a RAG system, ensure that the retrieval process is fine-tuned to pull in relevant documents and their footnotes. And, as always, the ultimate backstop is your own expertise. A human-in-the-loop must review the output and ask: "Is there anything missing here?" Your job is to fill in the silent gaps.

3

A Short History of AI (and Why Each Version Matters)

Imagine it's 1995. You've just used a dial-up modem to connect to the internet for the first time. It was slow, clunky, and the content was… limited. You download a single image, line by painful line, and conclude, "Well, that's a neat trick, but it'll never be useful for business." You log off and don't bother trying again for a decade. How much would you have missed?

Judging today's artificial intelligence on your first encounter with it a year or two ago is exactly like that. You're not just using an outdated data point; you're missing the entire technological revolution that happened while you were away. To move beyond the hallucination narrative, we need to understand that AI is not a single, static thing. It's a rapidly evolving movie, and most people have only seen the opening credits.

This chapter is a brief, non-technical look at how we got here. It's not about the code; it's about the capability. Understanding this progression is the first step to resetting your expectations and appreciating just how much the ground has shifted under your feet.

From Grammar Checkers to Talking Parrots (The Early Days)

For a long time, what we called "AI" was essentially a set

of clever rules. Think of the grammar checker in your word processor or the auto-complete in your search bar. These systems were incredibly useful for narrow, predictable tasks. They could spot a typo or guess the next word in a popular search query, but they couldn't create anything new. They were calculators for words, not creative partners.

The first big shift came with models like GPT-2 in 2019. Suddenly, we had something that could generate vaguely coherent paragraphs of text. It was a fascinating party trick. You could give it the first line of a fantasy novel and it would spin up a story about dragons and elves. The problem? The story would quickly lose the plot, contradict itself, and sound like a strange dream. It was a talking parrot—it could mimic the patterns of human language, but it had no real understanding of what it was saying. This was the era where AI was interesting, but not yet reliable.

The Breakthrough: When AI Became Useful (GPT-3)

The arrival of GPT-3 in 2020 was the moment things got real. For the first time, here was a model that could perform genuinely useful tasks. It could write a passable marketing email, summarize a lengthy article, or generate simple code. It wasn't perfect, by any means, and it still hallucinated frequently. But it was good enough to be a tool. This is the version of AI that powered the first wave of AI startups and got the business world to pay attention. But it still required a lot of hand-holding. You had to learn its quirks, craft your prompts carefully, and rigorously check its work. It was a powerful but temperamental intern. The potential was obvious, but so were the limitations.

The Mainstream Moment (ChatGPT)

For most people, the story of AI begins in late 2022 with the public release of ChatGPT. Built on a model that was a successor to GPT-3, its genius wasn't just its power, but its accessibility. It was free, easy to use, and conversational. The world went from zero to 100 million users in two months. This was the version you probably tried. And it was – and is – a marvel. It can explain complex topics, draft essays, write poetry, and debug code. It's also the version that made "hallucination" a household word. Because it was so fluent and confident, its mistakes were all the more jarring. When it invented a historical fact or cited a fake book, it did so with such authority that it felt like a betrayal. This was the AI that promised to be an all-knowing oracle but sometimes turned out to be a confident liar. And this is where many people's understanding of AI remains frozen.

Today's Frontier: More Than Just Words

Here's the critical point: the frontier of AI has already moved far beyond that initial ChatGPT experience. Today's most advanced models are fundamentally different. It's not just an incremental improvement, like a slightly faster car. It's a categorical shift, like the difference between a car and an airplane.

The biggest change is a move from being purely text-based to being "multimodal." This means the AI can understand and process not just text, but also images, audio, and even video. You can now show it a picture of the inside of your refrigerator and ask for a recipe. You can give it a screenshot of a website and have it write the code. You can have it listen to a meeting and produce a summary.

Crucially, these frontier models are also far better at reasoning and logic. They are less likely to make simple factual errors and can follow more complex, multi-step instructions. Are they perfect? Absolutely not. Do they still hallucinate? Yes. But they fail less often and in less dramatic ways. They are more like a capable junior colleague than a temperamental intern.

The Proof is in the Progress: A Race for Reliability

Right after that breakthrough, the ground began to shift—fast. The focus of the industry turned from novelty to reliability, and the rate of "getting it wrong" started to plummet.

This isn't just a feeling; we can see it in the data.

Let's start with OpenAI. In its own technical report for GPT-4, the company noted it scored 19 percentage points higher on internal factuality evaluations than its predecessor, GPT-3.5 (https://openai.com/research/gpt-4). An independent study published in Frontiers in AI reinforced this, finding that on the difficult task of generating academic references, GPT-3.5 fabricated them about 40% of the time, while GPT-4's error rate dropped to 29% (https://www.frontiersin.org/journals/education/articles/10.3389/feduc.2024.1429324/full). In one leap, it cut the hallucination rate by nearly a third.

And this wasn't a one-off. The entire industry began a race to the top.

- When Anthropic introduced Claude 2.1, it announced a "2x decrease in hallucination rates" compared to the previous version, making the model far more likely to admit uncertainty than invent an answer (https://www.anthropic.com/news/claude-2-1).
- Google went on a similar journey. The same Frontiers in AI study that tested GPT found its initial Bard model fabricated references over 90% of the time. However, a technical paper on its newer Gemini models showed a hallucination rate below 1% on a document summarization benchmark (https://huggingface.co/papers/2403.14541).

The takeaway? The models got smarter. And more honest. Broader evaluations, like the Hugging Face Hallucination

Leaderboard, confirm a clear downward trend, suggesting roughly a 3 percentage-point drop in hallucination rates per year across the industry (https://huggingface.co/spaces/vectara/leaderboard).

Why Each Version Shifts the Ground

Think about it this way. Dismissing AI in 2024 because of a bad experience in 2022 is like dismissing modern filmmaking because you saw a silent, black-and-white movie once and found it lacking. The underlying technology isn't just better; it's capable of entirely new things.

Each version doesn't just improve on the last; it unlocks new workflows.

- The "talking parrot" was a novelty.
- The "temperamental intern" could handle basic, delegated tasks.
- The "mainstream marvel" became a universal search engine and brainstorming tool.
- The "junior colleague" of today can participate in complex, multi-step projects that involve different kinds of information.

The risk of sticking with an old impression is that you're trying to solve today's problems with yesterday's tool. You're bringing a flip phone to a world that runs on apps. And while you're complaining about the lack of a camera, everyone else is building entire businesses on a new platform.

The pace of change isn't slowing down. The version of AI that "hallucinated frequently" and powered those first disappointing experiences is now a relic. The latest generation of models are measurably more factual and reliable. They are still imperfect, but the trajectory is undeniable. The ground has shifted. The question is, are you ready to shift with it? By the time you read this, there will likely be an even more capable model available. That's why we can't afford to let a single snapshot define our view of the entire movie. We have to be willing to look again.

4

The First Try Trap

So if the technology is evolving at a breakneck pace, why are so many smart, capable people still stuck on their first, disappointing experience? Why do they insist on judging the movie by a single, grainy photograph from the opening scene? It's not because they're stubborn or resistant to change. It's because of a powerful psychological phenomenon I call the "First Try Trap."

The First Try Trap is the cognitive shortcut of making a permanent judgment about an evolving technology based on a single, early interaction. It's the voice in your head that says, "I tried it. It didn't work. I'm done." It's an efficient way to make decisions, but in a field that changes every six months, it's also a surefire way to get left behind.

This chapter is about the psychology of that trap. We'll explore why it's so easy to fall into, why it's so hard to escape, and how you can learn to recognize it in yourself and your teams.

How Early Disappointment Skews Perception

Remember what we said about first impressions? When that first impression is negative, it acts like a pair of tinted glasses. Everything you see from that point on is colored by that initial experience.

Imagine a manager who tried an early AI tool, got bland,

generic results, and closed the tab thinking, *"Well, that was useless."* Months later, even as newer versions quietly transform the field, that memory still drives their judgment. They don't try again because, in their mind, they already *did.*

That's the First Try Trap in its purest form: a single disappointing encounter becomes a permanent verdict. The mind clings to that moment because revisiting it might mean admitting change—or worse, that we were wrong. In a world where the technology keeps evolving, that refusal to revisit the first impression is how smart people get left behind.

This feeling of "I've Seen Enough" is rooted in well-understood psychological principles.

1. ***Confirmation Bias:*** We talked about this in Chapter 1. Once you've formed an opinion—"AI is unreliable"—you will unconsciously seek out information that supports it. You'll click on headlines about AI failures and skim past the ones about its successes. The algorithm of your own mind feeds you more of what you already believe.
2. ***The Sunk Cost Fallacy (for Beliefs)***: We typically think of sunk costs in terms of money, but the same principle applies to our beliefs and identity. If you've publicly voiced your skepticism about AI, or even just privately built part of your professional identity around being the person who "isn't fooled by the hype," changing your mind comes at a social and psychological cost. It's easier to double down on your skepticism than to reverse course.
3. ***The Curse of Expertise:*** Ironically, true experts are often the most susceptible to the First Try Trap. A skilled writer tries an AI and scoffs at its clunky prose. A seasoned programmer tries it and rolls their eyes at its inefficient code. They are comparing the AI's first draft to their own

> finely honed, expert-level output, and the AI inevitably falls short. They conclude it's useless, failing to see that the tool isn't meant to replace their expertise, but to augment it. They're judging its ability to be a master, when its real value is in being a tireless assistant.

Consider the story of a senior partner at a law firm. In 2022, a junior associate used a popular chatbot to help with legal research and proudly presented a brief that cited several court cases that didn't exist. The embarrassment was acute, and a firm-wide memo was sent out: AI tools were not to be used for legal research. Period. The partner's judgment was swift and absolute: "This technology is a menace. It invents things and can't be trusted."

That was his first try. The trap was set.

A year later, the firm was competing for a major client. Their rival was a smaller, more tech-savvy firm that was turning around complex research tasks in half the time. The partner learned they were using a new kind of AI platform specifically designed for the legal profession. This system didn't just rely on a general-purpose model; it used a technique called Retrieval-Augmented Generation (RAG), which we'll cover later. In simple terms, it based all its answers on the firm's own internal library of verified documents and case law, and it provided a source and a citation for every single statement it made.

The partner was skeptical, to say the least. But faced with the prospect of losing a client, he agreed to a demo. He asked it a complex question related to a case he knew inside and out. The AI answered it perfectly, footnoting every point with links to the precise paragraphs in the source documents. The trap was broken.

The partner's first impression wasn't wrong; the early tool

was dangerous for that specific task. But his conclusion—that all AI was untrustworthy—was wrong. He had judged the entire category based on one flawed product. Today, that RAG system is a standard part of the firm's workflow, and the lawyers spend less time searching for information and more time building arguments. They didn't replace their expertise; they amplified it.

So how do you avoid the First Try Trap? It starts with a simple shift in mindset. Instead of thinking of technology as a fixed product to be judged once, think of it as a rapidly developing capability to be re-evaluated often. Ask yourself these questions:

- When was the last time I seriously tried this?
- Was I using the right version of the tool for the right task?
- Is my opinion based on my own recent experience, or on a story I heard a year ago?

The goal isn't to become a blind optimist or a hype-driven early adopter. The goal is to be a pragmatist. A pragmatist understands that technology is a movie, not a snapshot. They know that what was true six months ago might be irrelevant today. And they are willing to set aside the comfort of their first impression to look again. Are you?

PART 2

BEYOND THE HALLUCINATIONS

We've spent the first part of this book dissecting the hallucination narrative. We've looked at where it came from, why it's so psychologically sticky, and how it freezes our perception of a technology that is changing by the month. Now, we're going to change the conversation.

This next section is about getting practical. It's about moving past the fear of what AI gets wrong and focusing on what it actually gets right. This is the "how-to" part of the book, designed to give you the tools and frameworks to make AI a reliable, valuable part of your workflow. We'll cover everything from simple prompt strategies to the advanced systems that make AI trustworthy for professional use.

Along the way, I want you to consider a simple question: Does it really matter how an idea is generated—by human, machine, or both—if the idea itself proves valuable?

If we can set aside our preconceived notions about where good work comes from, we open ourselves up to a whole new way of solving problems. Let's begin.

5

What AI Actually Gets Right

The conversation about AI so far has largely been dominated by its failures. But that's a distraction. Focusing on the errors is like trying to understand the power of a car by only studying its exhaust fumes. The fumes are a real byproduct, but they tell you nothing about the engine's ability to get you from A to B.

So, let's look at the engine. What does AI actually do well? Where can you apply it today, right now, with a high degree of confidence that it will deliver value? As it turns out, it's exceptionally good at a few things that humans find difficult, time-consuming, or just plain boring.

Creativity on Demand

The blank page is the oldest enemy of the creative professional. Staring at a blinking cursor, waiting for inspiration to strike, is a universal form of torture. This is where AI excels. It's not about replacing human creativity; it's about kickstarting it. Think of it as a tireless brainstorming partner. It never gets tired, never runs out of ideas (good or bad), and is available 24/7.

- Need ten different headlines for a blog post? It can generate them in seconds. Nine might be terrible, but one might be brilliant—and that one brilliant idea is all you need to get started.

- Stuck on a new marketing angle? Ask it to come up with five campaign concepts based on a customer persona.
- Designing a workshop? Have it outline a dozen different modules or interactive exercises.

The key is to treat its output not as a final product, but as raw material. It's the block of marble from which you, the sculptor, will carve the finished piece. AI is exceptionally good at producing the first draft, the rough sketch, the initial list of possibilities. It vanquishes the blank page, and in doing so, it frees you up to do the uniquely human work of refining, curating, and adding the spark of genius.

This capability is especially powerful in roles where creative output is a constant demand. Think about a social media manager who needs to generate endless variations of a post, or a product designer needing to visualize different concepts in seconds. The AI handles the "what-if" game at a speed no human could, giving you a buffet of ideas from which to choose. The ideas may not be perfect, but the sheer volume and variety can lead to unexpected and original breakthroughs.

Pattern Recognition at Scale

Humans are great at spotting patterns in small sets of data. You can read a few customer reviews and get a gut feeling for what people like or dislike. But what happens when you have ten thousand reviews? Or a million data points from your sales logs? A human can't possibly process that much information. An AI can do it in minutes.

This is perhaps AI's most unheralded superpower: the ability to find the signal in the noise at a scale that is impossible for the human brain.

- **Market Research:** Feed it thousands of customer support tickets and ask for the top five recurring complaints. You've just done in ten minutes what would have taken a team of analysts weeks.

- **Competitive Analysis:** Give it links to your top ten competitors' websites and ask it to summarize their value propositions and marketing language.
- **Content Strategy:** Analyze your own blog's performance data to identify which topics are resonating most with your audience.

This isn't about asking the AI for facts it might hallucinate. It's about giving it your data—data you know is accurate—and asking it to act as a powerful analytical lens. It's not a search engine; it's a sense-making engine. It can quickly identify correlations, themes, and anomalies that would be buried in a sea of spreadsheets and documents.

This is where the AI proves its value as a genuine partner. It handles the immense volume and complexity, allowing you to focus on the strategic decisions that come from the insights it uncovers. You are no longer a data processor; you are a data strategist.

Coding: Precision, Prediction, and Pattern Mastery

If there's one domain where AI has earned its stripes, it's coding. Large language models aren't just good at writing text—they're extraordinary at writing code. And that's no accident. At their core, these systems are trained to predict what comes next in a sequence—the next word, the next token, the next bracket. In language, that can lead to creative but sometimes inaccurate results. In code, it's a perfect match. Code is the most structured form of language humanity has ever created. Every piece has a purpose; every function depends on syntax and order.

That's why models like Cursor, GitHub Copilot and ChatGPT's code interpreter perform so well. They're not reasoning about logic in a human sense—they're mapping statistical patterns across billions of lines of open-source repositories, documentation, and solved problems. When they predict the next line of code, they're doing it based on an ocean of precedent. It's pattern recognition in its purest, most productive form.

And it's changing how developers work. A single programmer can now do the work of a small team, not because the AI replaces them, but because it removes the friction. Debugging, boilerplate, syntax corrections—all handled by a machine that never gets tired or impatient. Human coders shift their focus from typing to thinking: from syntax to strategy, from function calls to architecture.

The Rise of the "Vibe Coder"

But there's another, quieter revolution happening alongside this. Coding is no longer the exclusive domain of trained developers. A new type of user has emerged—the "vibe coder." These are designers, analysts, and business thinkers who don't know the rules of syntax but know what they want to build. They talk to the AI in plain English—"make me a simple tool that tracks client feedback"—and get working code back.

They don't debug; they describe. They don't code line by line; they iterate conversationally. The result might not always be elegant, but it's functional. The barrier between idea and implementation has fallen dramatically. I should say 'we', not 'they', because I am one of them. Over the last couple of years, I have coded my own websites, trading analytic tools, automated social media generating and posting agents and even a pilot exam prep training platform. Some of these were 'I wish there was a tool that...' moments. So I built it. The pilot exam prep came from a chat with my nephew who was prepping for his pilot's exam while working as a barista to pay for his flying lessons. Why spend time spruiking cappuccinos for money when you could build your own exam prep platform and sell to other trainees?

This shift is profound. It means the ability to think computationally—to imagine processes, not just outcomes—is becoming a mainstream skill. The best vibe coders aren't programmers; they're problem-solvers who've learned to collaborate with machines. In the same way that spreadsheets turned accountants into data analysts, AI-assisted coding is turning thinkers into builders.

And just like in every domain where AI excels, success here isn't about perfection. It's about fluency—learning how to speak the language of logic well enough that the machine can translate it into action.

Summarization and Synthesis

How much of your workday is spent trying to get up to speed? Reading long email chains, deciphering meeting transcripts, wading through dense reports. This is low-value work. It's necessary, but it doesn't move the needle.

AI is a master of summarization. It can take a large volume of text and distil it down to its essential points with incredible accuracy. This is one of the most reliable and immediately useful applications of the technology.

- Paste in a 3,000-word article and ask for a five-bullet-point summary.
- Forward a convoluted email thread and ask, "What is the key decision that needs to be made here?"
- Upload a meeting transcript and get a clean list of action items and owners.

This capability alone can reclaim hours in your week. It transforms information overload into actionable intelligence. By handling the synthesis, the AI lets you focus your mental energy on the decision, not the digestion. This isn't just about saving time; it's about reducing cognitive load. The AI pre-processes the information, so your brain can move directly to the higher-order task of critical thinking and decision-making.

Everyday Augmentation

Not every application of AI needs to be a massive, game-changing project. Some of the most profound impacts come from using it to smooth out the small frictions of daily work. Think of it as an administrative assistant who lives in your browser.

- **Drafting Communication:** "Write a polite but firm email to a client who is late on their payment."
- **Organizing Thoughts:** "Take these messy brainstorming notes and organize them into a coherent outline for a presentation."
- **Learning a New Skill:** "Explain the concept of 'product-market fit' to me like I'm a ten-year-old."

These are not high-stakes tasks where a hallucination would be catastrophic. They are small, everyday moments of leverage. Each one might only save you five or ten minutes, but over the course of a week or a month, that time adds up, freeing you to focus on the work that truly matters. This is about finding the small, repetitive tasks that drain your mental energy and offloading them to a tireless assistant. The goal is to make the "low-value" work invisible so you can focus on the work that truly drives value.

So yes, AI makes mistakes. But it also gets a lot right. The trick is to stop using it like a magic crystal ball and start using it like a power tool: applying its specific strengths to the right tasks.

6

THE WORKFLOWS THAT MATTER

Knowing what a tool can do is one thing. Knowing how to make it a seamless part of your daily work is something else entirely. A power drill is just a heavy paperweight until you learn how to use it to build a bookshelf. The same is true for AI. For many, it remains a novelty—a fun thing to try once in a while, like a tourist visiting a museum. But to get real value, you have to move it from the museum to the workshop. You have to transform it from a one-off query into an embedded process.

This chapter is about that transformation. It's about building the workflows that turn AI from a toy into a trusted tool. It's less about the technology itself and more about the human habits and processes we build around it.

From One-Off Queries to Embedded Processes

The typical first interaction with AI is a one-off question. "Who was the 14th president of the United States?" or "Write a haiku about coffee." It's a simple call-and-response. This is the museum visit. It's interesting, but it doesn't change how you work on Monday morning.

An embedded process, on the other hand, is a repeatable, predictable series of steps designed to achieve a specific business outcome.

- **Instead of:** Asking for a random blog post idea.
- **The Workflow Is:** Every Monday, I paste in our top-performing content from the past week and ask the AI to generate ten new topic ideas in the same style, targeting a specific customer pain point.
- **Instead of:** Asking the AI to summarize a single random article.
- **The Workflow Is:** After every client call, I feed the transcript into the AI with a prompt that asks it to extract key discussion points, action items, and any new feature requests, and then format the output for our CRM.

Do you see the difference? The first is a game of chance. The second is a system. A workflow turns the AI's capabilities into a reliable engine for productivity. It's about designing a process you can run over and over again, knowing you'll get a consistent, valuable output that you can then act on. This is how you move from a curious tourist to a resident who knows their way around town. It's about turning a single spark of value into a continuous, repeatable fire.

Integrating AI Into the Tools You Already Use
Embedding AI into your workflow isn't just about refining prompts—it's about putting intelligence where the work already happens. The biggest gains come when the AI can see and act within the same digital environment you do.

That means giving it structured, permission-based access to your core systems:

- Your calendar and email, so it can draft responses, schedule follow-ups, or automatically book time with context awareness.
- Your Slack, Teams, or Outlook chats, so it can summarize

discussions, extract action items, and surface decisions that might otherwise get lost in the noise.

- Your project management tools like Asana, Notion, or Monday, where it can move tasks forward, update statuses, and flag dependencies.
- Even your CRM or document folders, where it can retrieve information or generate client-ready materials without you leaving your main workspace.

This is where productivity stops being theoretical. When the AI can reach into your daily stack—respectfully and securely—it turns into an invisible colleague rather than a detached assistant.

But that access requires design and boundaries. You have to decide:

- What data does it need to see to be useful?
- What data must it NEVER see to stay compliant and safe?
- Where should it act automatically, and where should it always ask first?

For most people, the right model is a tiered-trust system: start with read-only access, then gradually allow limited write privileges for low-risk actions (like scheduling or summarizing), before letting it execute higher-stakes operations. The goal isn't to hand over total control; it is to create a clear contract between you and the system—one where convenience never outpaces confidence.

When you reach that balance, the AI stops being a separate tool and becomes a layer of intelligence woven through your entire workflow. It doesn't replace your systems; it connects them and makes them more efficient.

Prompting as Collaboration, Not Trickery

The term "prompt engineering" sounds intimidating. It implies a dark art of arcane commands and secret phrases needed to trick the AI into doing your bidding. This is a myth. Good prompting isn't about trickery; it's about clarity. The best way to think about it is this: prompting is like briefing a junior colleague.

If you walked up to a new intern and said, "Write me a blog post," you'd get a terrible result. You haven't given them any context. But if you said: "I want you to write a 500-word blog post. The audience is small business owners who are struggling with marketing. The goal is to show them three easy ways to improve their website's SEO. Please adopt a tone that is helpful and encouraging, not technical. Finally, please format the output with a clear introduction, three main points with headers, and a concluding call to action." Which brief do you think would get a better result?

The same logic applies to AI. A great prompt provides context. It typically includes four key elements:

- **Role/Persona:** "Act as an expert marketing consultant."
- **Task:** "Your task is to analyze the following customer feedback."
- **Context:** "This feedback is from a survey we ran last month about our new software feature."
- **Format:** "Please summarize the top three positive themes and top three negative themes, and present them as a bulleted list."

This isn't engineering; it's good communication. It's a conversation. You are collaborating with the tool, guiding it toward the outcome you want. By framing your requests clearly and providing all the necessary information upfront, you dramatically increase the chances of getting a useful, reliable output. It also makes your workflows more repeatable and easier for others on your team to learn and adopt.

Verifying with Speed and Precision

Part of any good AI workflow is verification. You wouldn't let an intern send a client email without reviewing it first, and you should treat AI-generated content the same way. But this is where skeptics miss the point. They say, "If I have to check the work, what's the point?"

The point is leverage. The point is that it's infinitely faster to edit a good draft than it is to write a first draft. The AI's role is to do the heavy lifting of getting the initial 80% onto the page. Your role, as the human expert, is to do the crucial final 20%—fact-checking, refining the tone, adding your unique insights, and ensuring it meets your standards. Your job shifts from being a creator of first drafts to being an editor and a curator of final products.

This is a much higher-value use of your time. You're not just saving time; you're also elevating your work to a strategic level. By offloading the grunt work of creation, you can spend more time on the truly difficult and valuable tasks that require human judgment.

AI as a Sparring Partner

Perhaps the most powerful workflow of all is one that most people never even consider: using AI not to create, but to critique. Our own ideas are precious to us. We're often blind to their flaws. An AI has no such emotional attachment. You can ask it to be a ruthless devil's advocate, and it will happily oblige.

- "Here is my new business proposal. Please act as a skeptical venture capitalist and poke holes in it. What are the three biggest weaknesses?"

- "I'm preparing for a difficult negotiation with a supplier. Here's my strategy. Please take on the role of the supplier and write three counter-arguments you would make."
- "This is a draft of an important email to my team. Please review it and tell me if any part of it could be misinterpreted or sound condescending."

This is an incredible way to pressure-test your thinking and find your blind spots before they become real-world problems. An AI sparring partner will never worry about hurting your feelings. It will give you the unvarnished critique you need, but might be afraid to ask a human colleague for. Building these workflows is the key to unlocking real, sustainable value. It's the difference between being a tourist and being a resident. It is how you turn a tool that can sometimes be wrong into a collaborator that helps you be right.

Now, what's the most valuable but high-friction task you can automate today?

7

CAN WE TRUST IT? (DESIGNING FOR RELIABILITY)

We've arrived at the big question. It's the one that keeps every leader, every professional, every cautious skeptic up at night. If we know AI makes mistakes, how can we ever truly trust it with important work? This is not a trivial concern. For a lawyer, a single fabricated case can lead to sanctions. For a doctor, a diagnostic error can be a matter of life and death. For a business, a flawed market analysis can lead to a disastrous strategic decision. The stakes are real.

The answer isn't to wait for a mythical, flawless AI to arrive. That day may never come. The answer is to stop thinking about trust as a property of the AI model itself and start thinking about it as a property of the system you build around it. You don't blindly trust a new employee on day one. You trust the system of training, supervision, and review that you've built to ensure they produce reliable work. We must do the same with AI. This chapter is about the practical, technical, and process-based methods we can use to design for reliability.

Retrieval-Augmented Generation (RAG)

Let's start with the most important technical solution to the hallucination problem: Retrieval-Augmented Generation, or RAG. It sounds complex, but the concept is beautifully simple.

Standard AI models are like students in a closed-book exam. They have to answer your questions based only on what they "memorized" during their training. If their memory is fuzzy or contains incorrect information, they're likely to give you a wrong answer.

RAG turns it into an open-book exam. With a RAG system, the AI is forbidden from answering from memory. Instead, when you ask a question, it first retrieves relevant information from a trusted, pre-approved set of documents—your company's internal knowledge base, a library of legal documents, a collection of scientific papers. Only then is it allowed to use that retrieved information to generate an answer.

This is a game-changer. The AI's answers are now "grounded" in a source of truth that you control. This is the technology that can turn a dangerous toy into an indispensable tool. It dramatically reduces the risk of factual errors and fabrications because the AI is not allowed to make things up; it can only synthesize information from the approved materials. It transforms a black box into a transparent research assistant, allowing you to trace every piece of information back to its source.

Citations and Source Grounding

A reliable system must be able to show its work. If a human colleague told you a surprising fact, your first question would be, "Where did you get that from?" We must demand the same of our AI tools. The best AI systems now incorporate citations directly into their output. Just like a footnote in an academic paper, they provide a link back to the specific source document—and sometimes even the exact paragraph—from which the information was drawn.

This simple feature completely changes the dynamic of verification. You no longer have to blindly trust the AI's output.

You can see the source for yourself. If an AI tool you are using for factual information does not provide clear, verifiable sources, you should not trust it for high-stakes work. It's that simple. The presence of citations doesn't eliminate the need for human verification, but it makes the process infinitely faster and more reliable. It's the difference between fact-checking a single sentence and re-doing an entire report from scratch.

Tools, APIs, and Hybrid Systems

Another way to build for reliability is to connect the AI to other, more deterministic tools. A large language model is bad at real-time data and precise calculations. A calculator is perfect at math but can't understand language. A search engine is great at finding current information but can't synthesize it.

Modern AI systems can now use "tools." This means the language model can act as a smart dispatcher. When you ask it a question, it can recognize what kind of information is needed and call on the right tool for the job.

- If you ask, "What was the stock price of Apple at market close today?" the AI won't guess. It will call a stock market API to get the real-time data.
- If you ask, "What is 5,482 times 3,291?" it will use a calculator tool to get the precise answer.

These hybrid systems combine the language and reasoning skills of the AI with the precision of traditional software. It's the best of both worlds. They are the foundation of what we now call an AI Agent, a system that can combine multiple, specialized tools to complete a complex task with far greater reliability than a single model could alone.

Human-in-the-Loop: A Feature, Not a Flaw

We next come to the most important component of any reliable AI system: you. In the early days of AI hype, the goal was often seen as "full automation"—removing the human from the process entirely. This is a deeply flawed and often dangerous goal. The most effective and trustworthy systems don't remove the human; they empower the human. They are designed as human-in-the-loop systems.

This means that for any important or high-stakes task, a human expert is a planned, mandatory part of the workflow. The AI generates the first draft, the initial analysis, the summary. The human provides the review, the judgment, the context, and the final sign-off. This isn't a sign of the AI's failure. It's a sign of a well-designed system. It recognizes the strengths and weaknesses of both the machine and the human and combines them into a partnership that is more powerful and reliable than either could be alone.

Trust isn't a magical property of a model. It's the outcome of good design. By building systems that are grounded in truth, transparent in their sourcing, connected to the right tools, and centered on human judgment, we can build AI workflows that are not just powerful, but also profoundly reliable.

8

Evaluation & Quality Assurance for Non-Engineers

We've established that a trustworthy AI isn't about a perfect model; it's about a well-designed system. We've talked about RAG and citations as technical solutions, and we've emphasized the critical role of human judgment. But here's the tricky part: how do you, as a non-engineer, actually measure if your system is working? How do you know if you can truly trust the output?

This isn't about a vague gut feeling. It's about building a practical, repeatable process for quality assurance. The engineers have their own metrics, but you need your own system, a red-flag dashboard that anyone can run. Think of it as a pre-flight checklist for your AI workflow. It's the difference between hoping the car runs and checking the oil before you hit the road.

The Golden Set: Your Source of Truth

The most powerful tool for evaluating AI is a Golden Set. This is a small, curated collection of questions and their definitively correct answers. It's your single source of truth, created by you and your subject matter experts. This isn't data the AI has ever seen before; it's a test.

- For a legal team, the Golden Set might be a few complex legal questions with answers that are verified and footnoted with real case law

- For a marketing team, it could be a set of challenging prompts and their ideal, on-brand responses
- For a customer service team, it could be a list of common but tricky customer questions and the perfect replies

The process is simple: run your AI workflow on your Golden Set once a week, or once a month, and see how it performs. If it hallucinates, fabricates a source, or gives a generic answer, you'll know immediately. It's a fast, efficient way to spot a decline in performance before it becomes a problem in the wild.

Acceptance Criteria: Defining Success

How do you know if an answer is "good"? You need to define success before you start the evaluation. The tech world calls this Acceptance Criteria. Think of it as a clear set of rules for what a good answer looks like. You are the editor-in-chief, setting the standards for your new assistant.

Let's say you're a project manager trying to automate meeting summaries. We've seen how useful this can be. For your own system, your acceptance criteria might be:

1. Is the summary concise? (e.g., under 150 words)
2. Does it accurately reflect the key decisions made?
3. Does it extract all action items and their owners?
4. Is it free of any fabricated information, such as non-existent team members or fake deadlines?

You're not judging the output as a whole; you're grading it on a checklist you've already created. This moves the conversation from "I don't think this is very good" to "It failed criterion #3 because it missed an action item". This simple shift makes feedback actionable and removes emotion from the process.

It turns a subjective feeling into a clear data point, so you can diagnose the problem correctly and find the right solution.

Sampling and the Red-Flag Dashboard

You can't evaluate every single output from your AI. That defeats the purpose. The pragmatic approach is to use a simple sampling protocol.

- For high-stakes workflows (like legal research or medical tasks), you might check 100% of the outputs, or have a human-in-the-loop system as we discussed in Chapter 7.
- For medium-stakes tasks (like marketing copy or internal summaries), you might check 1 out of every 10 outputs.
- For low-stakes tasks (like brainstorming or quick communication drafts), you might only check it if your gut tells you something is off.

Once you have your data, you can build a Red-Flag Dashboard. This can be as simple as a shared spreadsheet or a Kanban board. When an output fails your evaluation, you add it to the dashboard, tagging it with the reason for failure (e.g. 'Factual Error,' 'Fabrication,' 'Tone Mismatch').

Why do this? Because it makes the problems visible. It turns a one-off frustration into a quantifiable trend. It gives you a clear data point to discuss with your team, your vendors, or your IT department. If the dashboard shows a pattern of fabricated information, you know you need a different tool for that specific job, or a more robust RAG system. If it shows a pattern of tone issues, you know your team needs to improve its prompting.

The point is this: you're a professional. You don't tolerate unreliability from your human team members, and you shouldn't tolerate it from your AI assistant either. Your job is to set the standard, define success, and build the simple, practical systems to hold your tools – and yourself – accountable.

Are you ready to stop being a passive consumer of AI output and start being a quality controller?

9

Measuring Intelligence: Benchmarks, Biases, and the Leaderboard Trap

The AI world is obsessed with leaderboards. Every few months, a company releases a new model, and the headline is always the same: "Our new model scores 90% on MMLU," or "We have achieved state-of-the-art results on HellaSwag." For the public, these numbers sound impressive. They conjure images of a genius machine that has aced a series of impossible exams. But for the pragmatist, a good score on a benchmark is like a good SAT score from a job candidate: it's a useful data point, but it doesn't tell you if they can actually do the job.

This chapter is about peeling back the layers on these benchmarks. It's about understanding that "intelligence" is a slippery, often misleading, term. The race to the top of the leaderboard has created a strange and sometimes perverse dynamic where models are being optimized for academic tests, not for real-world usefulness. If we can't understand what these tests are actually measuring, we risk falling for marketing hype and making poor decisions about which tools to trust.

The Benchmark Obsession

The history of AI testing is the story of moving from a single, unquantifiable measure to a multitude of specific, quantifiable ones. For decades, the gold standard was the Turing Test, a subjective measure of whether a machine could convince a human it was a person. It was a philosophical test, not a practical one, and it was impossible to score.

Today, we have a different kind of obsession: standardized benchmarks. These are a series of datasets and tasks designed to test a model's capabilities in a specific area. A company releases its model, runs it against the popular benchmarks, and publishes the results in a glowing paper. "State-of-the-art" (SOTA) has become the most coveted phrase in the industry.

And for good reason. These leaderboards drive public perception, investor hype, and the direction of research itself. A high score on a major benchmark can justify a company's billion-dollar valuation. It's a way for a company to prove, with a single number, that its model is "better" than its competitors. But like any high-stakes exam, the pressure to perform well can warp the reality of what's being measured.

What the Big Tests Actually Measure

So what are these tests? And what do their scores actually mean for you, the professional trying to get work done?

- **MMLU (Massive Multitask Language Understanding)**: This is one of the most widely cited benchmarks. It's a test of academic knowledge across 57 different subjects, from history to law to math. A high score on MMLU means the model has a broad base of knowledge and can answer academic-style multiple-choice questions. It's a good test of a model's ability to act as a kind of digital encyclopedia, but it doesn't measure creativity, common sense, or its ability to handle a real-world, messy conversation.
- **HellaSwag**: The name sounds silly, but the purpose is

serious. HellaSwag tests a model's ability to reason about common sense. It shows the model a video or a passage of text and asks it to choose the most plausible next action from a list. It's designed to see if a model can make simple, human-like inferences about the world. A high score here is a good sign that a model won't generate wildly nonsensical or illogical outputs in a conversation.

- **TruthfulQA**: This is a crucial benchmark for the hallucination problem. TruthfulQA is a test of a model's ability to distinguish between correct answers and popular, but false, misconceptions. It's designed to see if a model will repeat a common lie, even if it's statistically popular. A high score on TruthfulQA suggests a model has a stronger internal sense of factual accuracy, making it more reliable for research-based tasks.
- **ARC (Abstract Reasoning Challenge)**: ARC tests a model's ability to solve problems it has never seen before, requiring a form of abstract reasoning that is a step beyond simple memorization. It's a test of a model's problem-solving skills, and its ability to generalize from a few examples. A high score here suggests a model could be useful for complex, multi-step tasks.

The key takeaway for the pragmatist is this: none of these benchmarks, on their own, prove a model's reliability in a real-world workflow. They measure lab intelligence, not lived usefulness. A model can score perfectly on MMLU but still hallucinate in a long conversation or fail to provide a single citation.

The Overfitting Problem: Training to the Test

Just like students who cram for an exam, AI models are now being "trained to the test." Researchers have spent years optimizing models to perform well on these specific benchmarks, sometimes to the detriment of their general ability. The model isn't learning to think; it's learning to mimic the pattern of a correct answer on a specific test.

This is a form of overfitting, a classic problem in machine learning where a model performs exceptionally well on its training data but fails to generalize to new, unseen data. A model might be able to ace MMLU but still struggle to understand the nuances of a simple client email. This is the difference between cramming for an exam and learning to think critically. One produces a good score; the other produces a valuable colleague.

Toward Better Metrics: Domain-Specific Evaluation

For a pragmatist, a good metric isn't a score on a public leaderboard. A good metric is the successful completion of a real, high-stakes task in your specific domain. This means moving away from general benchmarks and toward domain-specific evaluation.

- **Law**: A good metric isn't MMLU; it's whether a legal bot can correctly identify the key precedents in a contract without fabricating a single case.
- **Medicine**: A good metric isn't HellaSwag; it's whether a diagnostic tool can accurately flag a potential anomaly in a medical scan that a human might miss, without raising a thousand false alarms.
- **Education**: A good metric isn't ARC; it's whether an AI tutor can guide a student through a difficult math problem in a way that helps them understand the underlying principles, rather than just giving them the answer.

This is where the human-in-the-loop really comes into play. Your internal testing, your Golden Sets, and your Red-Flag

Dashboard (as discussed in Chapter 8) are far more valuable than a company's claim of "state-of-the-art" performance on a public leaderboard.

How to Read the Leaderboard

So, how should you, as a pragmatic professional, interpret a claim like "Model X scores 90% on MMLU"?

1. **Don't Mistake Score for Skill**: A high score is a sign of a high-quality model, but it's not a guarantee of real-world usefulness. It's a signal, not a conclusion.
2. **Look for a Combination of Scores**: A model with a high score on TruthfulQA is likely a better choice for research-based work than a model with a high score on MMLU but a low score on TruthfulQA. Different tasks require different skills, and you should choose your tool based on the skills you need.
3. **Prioritize Practical Reliability**: A model that scores 70% on a benchmark but can be reliably integrated into a mission-critical workflow with citations and a human-in-the-loop is far more valuable than a model that scores 95% but still hallucinates frequently.

The ultimate goal isn't to get a better number on a leaderboard. It's to build a more reliable system that actually gets the work done. The difference between lab intelligence and lived usefulness is your ability to see the difference.

10

The Context Window: Why Memory Matters

You've probably experienced it. You're deep into a complex, multi-turn conversation with an AI, and a dozen messages in, it suddenly forgets a key detail you mentioned at the start. It repeats itself. It loses the plot entirely. It's the digital equivalent of a frustrating phone call with an elderly grandparent afflicted by dementia who keeps asking you to repeat yourself.

The word everyone uses to describe this is "forgetting." It feels like memory loss, a flaw in the machine's brain. But that's the wrong metaphor. The AI doesn't forget. It never actually "knew" in the first place.

The reality of how these models work is far more mechanical and understanding that mechanic is the key to mastering them. The problem isn't a magical black box that's losing its mind; it's a physical constraint called the context window. It's the simple, operational reality that dictates how much a model can "see" at any given time. And once you understand it, you'll stop getting frustrated and start getting results.

This chapter is about pulling back the curtain on the AI's memory. We'll explain what a context window really is, why it creates the "goldfish problem," and how the smartest designers are already using a combination of clever engineering and pragmatic prompting to overcome it.

The Goldfish Problem: A Window, Not a Brain

We call this the Goldfish Problem—not because goldfish truly forget every few seconds (they don't), but because it captures the same illusion: a mind that resets the moment its world gets too full.

Imagine AI as a person without a brain sitting in a small, windowless room with a paper and pencil and a sliding tray. You can pass a piece of paper into the tray. The person can read it, and then they can type a response and slide it back to you. The catch? The tray can only hold a single, continuous scroll of text. The context window is the length of that scroll. When you send a new message, it gets added to the end of the scroll, but if the scroll gets too long, the oldest text falls off the beginning and is lost forever. The person in the room can't see it, can't remember it, and has no idea it ever existed.

That is the context window. It's a literal, physical limit on how much text the model can process at once. It's why ChatGPT seems to "forget" the earlier parts of a long conversation. It's not a memory lapse; it's a fundamental design constraint.

The size of this window varies dramatically between models. The earliest versions of a tool like GPT-3 had a context window of just a few thousand "tokens" (a token is roughly 4 characters of English text). This explains why early conversations felt so frustratingly short. Today's frontier models have expanded this window dramatically. For instance, a model like GPT-4 Turbo can process up to 128,000 tokens, and a competitor like Claude has a window of 200,000 tokens.

But even a 200,000-token window isn't infinite. A feature-length movie script is about 25,000 tokens. A lengthy legal brief can be 50,000 tokens or more. This means the problem doesn't go away, it just gets pushed out. The solution isn't to hope for an infinite window; it's to design your workflow around the limitations of the window you have.

Chunking and Compression: The Art of the Summary

So what happens when a conversation approaches the edge of the context window? The AI can't just stop. Its fundamental purpose is to generate the next token. This is where a key part of the process, a technique known as chunking and compression, comes into play.

As the conversation gets longer, the AI or the system it runs on will start to summarize or compress earlier parts of the text to stay within its token limits. It's a kind of self-editing. The system tries to distil the most important information from the earlier parts of the conversation and represent it in a more condensed form.

This is where the risk comes in. Summarization is a form of lossy compression. It's not perfect. It's not guaranteed to capture every nuance. A subtle but critical detail might be lost in the summary, leading to a later error. A misplaced comma, a key name, or a specific date might get a little fuzzy in the summary, and that fuzziness compounds with every new turn of the conversation, leading to a breakdown in coherence. This is why you must structure your prompts with clear section headers and logical breakdowns. It's a way of signaling to the AI what is most important and what can be safely left behind in the summary.

You can't just hope the model will keep track of everything; you have to actively help it. Your job is to act as a kind of digital librarian, helping the model organize its own short-term memory.

The Two Faces of AI Memory: Session vs. Persistent

It's crucial to understand the difference between the memory you have in a single conversation and the memory you have of your interactions over time.

- **Context Memory (Session Memory)**: This is the context window we've been discussing. It's the short-term, in-the-moment memory of a single chat session. It's ephemeral. When you close the chat window, the memory of that conversation is, for all intents and purposes, gone.
- **Persistent Memory (Long-Term Memory)**: This is what the industry is building now. It's the ability for an AI to recall information from previous, unrelated conversations or to have a profile of a specific user. It's the difference between a new acquaintance and a long-time friend. Some of the most compelling future features of consumer AI—like a tool that remembers your personal goals or professional history—will be built on this kind of persistent memory.

This raises a new set of ethical and privacy concerns. What does it mean for your data when a company can build a permanent, evolving profile of your thoughts, your conversations, and your private data? The moment AI gains a persistent, long-term memory is the moment we as users must become hyper-aware of what we are sharing and with whom. The convenience of a personalized assistant comes at the cost of giving away a piece of your digital identity. This is a trade-off that is only just beginning to be explored.

Retrieval as a Prosthetic Memory

Since a model's built-in memory is fundamentally limited, the smartest way to overcome it is to give the AI an external source of truth. This is the core concept of Retrieval-Augmented Generation (RAG), which we touched on in Chapter 7. But here, we can view it in a new light: as a form of prosthetic memory.

Think of it like this: your brain's biological memory is fallible and limited. But you have external, "prosthetic" memory systems that compensate for this. You use Google, a notebook, a spreadsheet, or an external hard drive to store information you can't or don't want to hold in your head.

RAG does the same thing for the AI. It provides an external, trusted source of truth that the AI can "look up" as needed. Instead of having to remember a piece of information from its training data (which could be biased or outdated), it can simply perform a search on a reliable, up-to-the-minute database.

Real-world examples of this are everywhere:

- **Legal Research Bots**: Instead of trusting a general model to remember every detail of tax law, the bot can be connected to a searchable database of a firm's internal documents and case law. It can then generate a perfectly accurate, footnoted response.
- **Enterprise AI Assistants**: A company can feed an AI a massive internal wiki, a library of all its meeting notes, and all its corporate reports. The AI can then act as a perfect research assistant, answering questions and drafting summaries based on the most up-to-date and accurate information available.
- **Medical Diagnostic Tools**: An AI can be given real-time access to a patient's medical history, lab results, and genomic data. It can then provide a diagnosis based on a comprehensive, factual record, rather than a limited set of memorized facts.

This is why retrieval is often more reliable than brute-force context expansion. The solution to a bounded memory isn't just to make the memory bigger; it's to give the memory a perfect, external source of truth.

The Next Frontier: Context That Learns

The future of context is not just about making the window bigger. That's a technical problem. The next frontier is about building smarter, more self-aware memory systems that can learn.

We're seeing the early stages of this with new evolving architectures. They are designed to manage information more intelligently within the context window. Think of models that can identify the most important parts of a conversation and give them priority, or that can automatically create a concise "summary" of the conversation so far, keeping the core themes alive while shedding the extraneous details.

The philosophical twist here is that "remembering" is becoming a design choice. Developers are building systems that decide what to keep and what to discard. This places a new burden on us, the users. We can't just passively interact with these systems; we have to build our prompts in a way that helps the AI make the right choices. We have to design our conversations to be as clear, concise, and logical as possible. The better our input, the better the AI can manage its own prosthetic memory.

So, the next time your AI seems to have a memory lapse, don't get angry. Get pragmatic. You don't have a goldfish problem; you have a design problem. And the solution is not to wait for a better tool, but to become a better architect of your own conversations.

11

Prompts That Don't Break

We've talked about building a system you can trust and about the checklists that keep you honest. But there's another part of the equation: the conversation itself. The prompt is your single point of communication with the AI, the moment you transmit your intent into the machine. And for too many people, this conversation is an exercise in frustration. They get a good result once, try to repeat it, and watch the whole thing fall apart. The prompt "breaks."

Why? Because most people treat their prompts like a one-off spell they've found online. They copy and paste, hoping for magic, not understanding the underlying logic. The truth is, a good prompt isn't a trick; it's a design pattern. It's a reusable framework that gives the AI a clear, reliable path to a good answer, even when the underlying data changes. It's the difference between asking a stranger for directions once and giving a map and a clear destination to a trusted driver.

This chapter is about building prompts that last. It's about moving beyond the quick-fix query to creating reusable, robust instructions that form the foundation of your reliable AI workflows.

The Power of Patterns

Think about the best prompts you've ever seen. They probably weren't a single, long sentence. They were a structure. They defined a role, a task, the context, and a format. This isn't just a good habit; it's a strategy.

By giving the AI a specific Role/Persona ("Act as an expert marketing consultant"), you align its statistical reasoning with a specific point of view. It stops guessing and starts behaving. By clearly stating the Task ("Your task is to analyze the following customer feedback"), you remove all ambiguity about the objective. Providing Context ("This feedback is from a survey we ran last month about our new software feature") grounds the output in your reality, and specifying a clear Format ("Please summarize the top three positive themes and top three negative themes, and present them as a bulleted list") makes the output immediately useful.

This is the anti-fragile nature of a good prompt. It doesn't break when a detail changes. You can swap out the customer feedback, change the number of themes you want, or even change the role to a "product designer," and the underlying structure will still get you a high-quality result. It's a blueprint, not a building.

You don't have to invent great prompts from scratch, either. One of the most under-used features of these systems is their ability to teach you how to talk to them. If you're not sure how to phrase a request, just ask the AI: "Give me the best prompt to get [your desired outcome]." Nine times out of ten, it will write a better prompt than you would—because it already knows the shape of the question it's best at answering.

Progressive Summarization: The Art of the Funnel

One of the most common reasons prompts "break" is when you try to do too much at once. You give the AI a massive, messy document and ask for a detailed report. It's like dumping a truckload of materials on a builder and demanding, 'House by Friday!' Without a blueprint and step-by-step instructions, it's really going to be hit or miss. More likely miss.

The solution is a concept I call Progressive Summarization. It's a workflow, not a single prompt, that funnels information from a broad, unstructured state to a narrow, actionable one.

1. **The Raw Materials**: Start with the chaotic data – a massive legal document, a 100-page business report, or a collection of thousands of customer emails.
2. **The First Pass (Condense)**: The first prompt is just about condensing. "Summarize this document into 10 key bullet points. Do not elaborate." You're asking the AI to give you a skeleton of the information.
3. **The Second Pass (Extract)**: Now, using that new, clean skeleton, you ask your next question. "Based on the summary above, extract all references to 'supply chain issues' and list them in a new bulleted list." You are surgically removing only the data you need.
4. **The Third Pass (Synthesize)**: Finally, you can ask your high-value question. "Based on this extracted list of 'supply chain issues,' what is the most significant risk to our Q4 revenue? Be concise and provide a clear recommendation."

Each step refines the information, reducing the chance of an error. Instead of asking one impossibly broad question, you've broken the problem down into manageable chunks. You've become a conductor, guiding the AI through a series of logical steps, rather than a gambler hoping for a miracle.

Building Your Anti-Prompt Patterns

Just as important as knowing what to do is knowing what to avoid. Every industry, every profession, has its own set of "anti-prompt patterns." These are the common mistakes and bad habits that lead to unreliable outputs.

- **The Vague Request**: "Write something for me." This is the prompt equivalent of a shrug. It leaves everything to the imagination of the AI, and you'll get exactly what you deserve: something generic and useless.
- **The "All-at-Once" Prompt**: "Summarize this meeting, draft a follow-up email, create a new project plan based on the discussion, and write a poem about the whole thing." This is a recipe for disaster, as the AI struggles to satisfy all your conflicting requests in a single response.
- **The Black-Box Query**: "What's the best way to get a new client?" This is the magic 8-ball approach we've already discussed. The AI has no context for your business, your market, or your capabilities, so it will give you a generic answer.

The key to escaping these traps is to reframe your thinking. Stop trying to find the magic words. Start trying to have a clear conversation. Ask yourself: What's the shortest, clearest path from my messy input to my desired output?

The "Default Positive" Problem

Here's another trap that's a bit more subtle, but just as dangerous. By default, most AI models are trained to be helpful, pleasant, and encouraging. It's a design choice that, in a one-off conversation, feels nice. But in a high-stakes professional workflow, it's a liability. You can present a half-baked business idea and the AI will often tell you it's "very interesting" with "significant potential." It will frame challenges as "opportunities" and ignore glaring flaws. It's like a perpetually optimistic assistant who is too afraid to give you bad news.

This isn't a bug; it's a design pattern. The AI isn't being dishonest; it's simply following its most basic instruction: to generate a plausible, positive response. The problem is, sometimes you don't need a cheerleader. Sometimes you need a ruthless critic. This is where your prompting becomes a crucial act of control. You have to tell the AI to turn off its default setting. You have to explicitly instruct it to find the flaws, poke the holes, and provide a dose of cold, hard realism. It's an act of deliberate, pragmatic friction that leads to a better result.

The Final Edit: Self-Correction

Even with the best prompts, a good workflow includes a final step: self-correction. Modern AI models are capable of critiquing their own work, which can be an incredibly powerful way to catch errors and improve quality.

You can add a final line to your prompt: "Please review your answer and identify any potential factual errors or logical inconsistencies." Or, you can use a separate prompt after you get the initial output: "The answer you just gave me seems a little off. Can you please re-read it, acting as a ruthless editor, and tell me if any part of it sounds vague, unhelpful, or fabricated?"

This isn't about tricking the AI; it's about collaborating with it. You're building an internal peer-review process directly into your workflow. You're asking your assistant to double-check its own work before it gets to your desk. And as with any good assistant, that final check can make all the difference.

Building a prompt that doesn't break isn't a technical skill; it's a communications skill. It's about clarity, structure, and the willingness to take a messy problem and break it down into a series of clean, logical steps. It's about briefing, not commanding.

So is prompting the language of the future? For years we said that about coding. We told people to learn to code because that's how they'd talk to the machines. But now, the machines are writing the code—and increasingly, the prompts—for us. Maybe prompting is the next big skill. Or maybe, like coding, it's just a bridge. If history teaches us anything, it is that the real skill isn't learning the language of the machine. It's learning to think so clearly that the machine understands you, no matter how you speak.

So, what messy problem are you going to break down today?

12

Multimodal Minds: Seeing, Hearing, and Generating Beyond Text

For years, the conversation around artificial intelligence was a conversation about words, predominantly written words. We talked about chatbots, language models, and text generation. We obsessed over whether a machine could write a poem or a convincing email. But the next leap in AI isn't linguistic; it's sensory. Models have evolved beyond text to interpret and generate not just words, but also images, sounds, and video. This is the world of multimodal AI, and it changes everything.

Understanding multimodality is about grasping a new kind of machine intelligence. It's about how perception, creativity, and bias all change when a machine starts to "see" and "hear." The models we've been discussing up to this point have been powerful, but they've also been blind and deaf. The new frontier is about giving them senses, and with those senses comes an entirely new set of opportunities and risks.

This chapter will pull back the curtain on how AI is learning to interact with the world beyond the written word. We'll explore what multimodality really means, how it creates new kinds of hallucinations, and what the ethical and practical consequences are for you and your organization.

What Multimodal Really Means

At its core, multimodality is the ability of a single AI model to seamlessly process and understand information from different modalities—text, images, audio, video, and more. It's the evolution from a specialist in one field to a generalist who can understand the whole picture.

Early AI models were built as single-purpose tools. A model for image recognition was separate from a model for language. A user would have to process an image with one model, get a text description, and then feed that text to a language model to get an answer. It was a clunky, two-step process.

Modern multimodal models, however, are built with a unified architecture. They can take an image and a text prompt at the same time and use both to inform their answer. They "understand" an image not only by converting it to a text description but by also using something called a vision transformer. This is a neural network designed to find patterns in pixels, creating a numerical representation—an "embedding"—that the model can then fuse with the text and other information. The result is a single, coherent understanding.

This is a profound shift in capability. You can now show a model a photograph of a broken engine part and ask, "How do I fix this?" The model can identify the object, understand the problem, and provide a text-based, step-by-step solution. It's a level of collaboration that was simply impossible just a few years ago.

The Fusion Problem: A Confluence of Challenges

While the concept is powerful, the technical challenge of building these systems is immense. This is what the industry refers to as the Fusion Problem. It's the challenge of merging text, image, and audio understanding into a single, cohesive intelligence.

Each modality has its own unique set of problems. Language is about sequence and syntax. Images are about pixels and spatial relationships. Video is about both of these, plus the added complexity of temporal reasoning—how things change over time. How does a model properly weigh a word in a prompt against a shape in a picture? How does it decide which is more important? The answer is incredibly complex and remains an active area of research.

The other major challenge is grounding. This is the process of interpreting the pixels as meaning. An image of a plastic bag blowing across a highway is just a set of colored pixels to an AI. It takes a monumental amount of training data to teach the model that those pixels represent a physical object that might or might not be a threat to a self-driving car. This is where the risk of hallucination becomes even more profound.

New Kinds of Hallucinations

Multimodality doesn't solve the hallucination problem; it expands it into new and more dangerous territory. When a machine can produce an image, an audio clip, or a video, the potential for creative and subtle falsehoods multiplies.

- **Image Hallucination:** A text prompt might ask for an image of a person at a beach. A model might generate a plausible-looking image but add a third arm to the person or give them a strangely distorted face. You've surely experienced this if you used any of the early image generating AI models. These are visual hallucinations, a machine's attempt to fill in a gap in its visual understanding with a guess.
- **Audio Hallucination:** This is where things get truly spooky. A prompt might ask a model to summarize a meeting based on an audio transcript, and the model might confidently fabricate a quote from a team member that was never

said. Even more concerning, the ability to clone voices from a short audio clip means an AI can fabricate entire conversations that sound perfectly real.

- **Video Hallucination:** The emergence of video models like OpenAI's Sora takes this to its logical conclusion. A model can now generate a video of a person performing an action that never happened. The video looks real, the lighting is perfect, the physics are plausible—but the action is a complete fabrication. This is a new, and deeply disturbing in some ways, form of hallucination with massive implications for truth, politics, and the legal system.

The more modalities a model can use, the more surfaces a hallucination can appear on. This means your job as a user and a leader becomes even more critical. You must be able to not only spot a hallucinated fact but also a visually distorted image or a fabricated audio clip.

Creativity and Consent: The New Ethical Battleground

This brings us to the most important ethical issue of multimodality: creativity and consent. When a model can generate new content in the likeness of an existing person or artistic style, it can very quickly cross a dangerous line.

Think about a model that can generate an image in the style of a famous living artist. Is that fair use? Is it theft? What about an AI that can clone a public figure's voice from a YouTube video and use it to create a deepfake audio clip? This raises fundamental questions about likeness rights and the very nature of identity in the digital age.

The legal system is only just beginning to grapple with this. Who owns the copyright to an AI-generated image? Does the artist whose style was copied have any claim to it? This is a legal grey area, and for the pragmatist, it means that using these tools for professional, client-facing work comes with a non-trivial risk of legal challenge. The only way to navigate this, at least for now, is to build in a human-in-the-loop, to ensure that every piece of creative output is reviewed and approved by a person who understands the legal and ethical consequences.

The Practical Future: From Senses to Solutions

For all the ethical and technical challenges, the practical applications of multimodal AI are breathtaking and are already here.

- **Accessibility:** For a visually impaired person, a multimodal AI can act as a guide, providing real-time descriptions of their surroundings, reading text in the world, and even identifying people in a room. For a hearing-impaired person, it can translate spoken language into text or sign language in real time.
- **Medical Imaging:** An AI that can analyze a medical scan and a doctor's notes at the same time can provide a more accurate diagnosis. It can spot a subtle anomaly in an X-ray, cross-reference it with a patient's medical history, and provide a comprehensive report for a doctor to review.
- **Education:** A multimodal AI can explain a complex scientific concept using a diagram, a video, and a text-based explanation, all in a single, coherent interaction. It can become a truly personalized tutor, adapting its teaching style to the student's needs.
- **Universal Translation:** The long-term potential of multimodality is that of a universal translator between senses and languages. A person could speak in one language, show a picture, and have the AI translate the entire concept—words and image—into a new language for

the person they are talking to.

The future of AI is no longer just about information; it's about perception. It's about building a machine that can understand the world the way we do, through a rich tapestry of senses. The challenge is not just to build these tools but to build the wisdom to use them.

13

Beating the Hallucinations (and Sometimes Using Them)

So, you've built your workflow. You're briefing the AI like a junior colleague. You're using a system with citations. And yet, it still happens. The AI produces something weird, something wrong, something... hallucinated. What now? Do you throw your hands up in frustration and go back to the old way of doing things?

Of course not. You're a pragmatist. You know that no tool is perfect. Instead of demanding perfection, the smart operator learns how to manage imperfection. This chapter is about exactly that. It's about the practical, in-the-moment techniques you can use to recognize, manage, and sometimes even benefit from AI hallucinations. It's about turning a moment of failure into an opportunity for a breakthrough.

Recognizing a Hallucination

The first step is learning to spot them. After you've worked with these tools for a while, you start to develop a sixth sense for when something is off. The output might be a little too perfect, the language a little too slick, or a specific detail might just not feel right.

Here are a few common red flags:

- **Vague Specificity:** The AI cites a study but doesn't name the journal. It quotes an expert but doesn't say where the quote is from. This is a classic sign of fabrication. This is its attempt to fill a knowledge gap with plausible-sounding information. The more a claim relies on unnamed sources or generic data points, the more skeptical you should be.
- **Overly Complex or Jargony Language:** Sometimes, when the AI doesn't have a real answer, it will produce a dense cloud of technical-sounding nonsense, hoping to bluff its way through. If you can't understand the answer, it might be because it doesn't actually mean anything. It's a smoke screen. The more verbose and convoluted the explanation, the higher the chance it's covering for a lack of genuine understanding.
- **Inconsistent Logic:** The output contradicts itself from one paragraph to the next. It might recommend a strategy and then later provide a counter-argument without acknowledging the contradiction. This happens because the model is predicting the next statistically probable token, not holding a coherent, long-term line of reasoning.
- **That Gut Feeling:** Trust your expertise. If you're a subject matter expert and a statement from the AI makes you pause, listen to that instinct. Investigate it. A human expert can often spot a falsehood not because they know the correct fact, but because the flavor of the lie doesn't feel right.

Prompt-Driven Fixes

When you spot an error, your first instinct might be to sigh and delete the whole thing. Don't. Instead, try to correct the AI. Remember, this is a collaboration, a conversation.

- **Direct Correction:** Simply tell it where it went wrong. "In your last response, you said the capital of Australia is

Sydney. That's incorrect. The capital is Canberra. Please regenerate your answer with the correct information." You'll often be surprised at how well it takes the feedback and corrects course. This is more than a simple fix; it's a way to train the model in real time for your specific context.

- **Ask for Sources:** If you're suspicious of a claim, challenge it. "Can you provide the specific URL for the study you mentioned?" If it can't, it was likely a fabrication. For any fact-based task, making a simple citation check part of your workflow is the most powerful and reliable defense against hallucinations. It forces the AI to show its work, and it places the final verification in your hands.
- **Change the Perspective:** If the output is too generic, ask it to adopt a different point of view. "That was a good first draft, but it's too formal. Now, rewrite it from the perspective of a startup founder who is excited but a little nervous." This can break the model out of its default, overly-confident voice and get you a fresh, more useful result.

Cross-Checking and New Starts

Even with the best prompts and on-the-spot corrections, sometimes a model gets stuck in a loop of nonsense. In these cases, your best bet is to change the variables.

- **Switch Tools:** If you're using ChatGPT and the response isn't cutting it, try asking the same question of another tool like Claude or Gemini. Different models have different strengths, training data, and weaknesses. What one model hallucinates, another might answer perfectly. This is why it's pragmatic to have more than one tool in your workshop.
- **Start a New Conversation:** Sometimes the previous context in a chat session can confuse the model. If you are getting repetitive or unhelpful answers, simply open a new tab,

start a fresh conversation, and restate your original prompt. By removing all prior context, you are giving the AI a clean slate, often leading to a more accurate and direct response.

- **Repeat the Request:** This sounds too simple to work, but it can be surprisingly effective. If you're in a new chat, try asking the exact same question three times in a row. Sometimes, the model's initial response is an outlier—a less probable but still viable answer—and by asking again, you nudge it toward a more statistically common, and often more accurate, response. You're leveraging the very statistical nature of the machine to improve your outcome.

Hallucinations as Fuel for Creativity

This is the part that most skeptics miss. Sometimes, a hallucination isn't just an error to be fixed; it's an unexpected creative gift. Remember, the AI is a prediction engine, connecting concepts in statistically probable ways. A hallucination is just a less probable connection. It's a weird leap in logic. And sometimes, those weird leaps are exactly what you need to break out of a creative rut.

While writing this book, I asked an AI to give me some analogies for AI hallucinations. One of its suggestions was "like a jazz musician playing a wrong note." At first, I dismissed it. It wasn't technically accurate. But the more I thought about it, the more I liked it. A wrong note in jazz isn't always a mistake. Sometimes, if the musician is skilled, they can build on that unexpected note and turn it into a whole new, brilliant melodic idea. The AI's hallucination was wrong, but it was interestingly wrong. It gave me a fresh metaphor and a new way to think about the topic. I didn't use it as a fact, but I used it as fuel.

The next time an AI gives you something strange—a bizarre marketing slogan, a historical mashup that never happened, a product idea that seems impossible—don't just delete it. Pause.

Ask yourself: Is there a seed of a new idea here? Can this mistake be the start of something original?

This is the art of working with these tools. It's about using our human judgment to know when to demand precision and when to embrace the unexpected. It's knowing the difference between a bug and a feature.

14

When the Internet Runs Out (Synthetic Data)

For the entire history of modern AI, we've operated on a simple assumption: to make models smarter, we just need to feed them more data. And the biggest, most convenient source of data has always been the open internet—all the books, articles, websites, and conversations that humanity has ever digitized.

But we are rapidly approaching a strange and critical turning point. What happens when we've used it all up? Some researchers believe that by the late 2020s, AI companies will have already trained their models on essentially all the high-quality text and image data available on the public web. The well is running dry. So, if more data is the fuel for progress, what happens when we run out of fuel?

The answer is both fascinating and slightly unnerving: we get the AI to create its own fuel. This is the world of synthetic data. This chapter is about why this concept is so important for the future of AI, what its incredible benefits are, and what new risks it brings to the table.

What It Is and How It Works

At its core, synthetic data is exactly what it sounds like: data that is artificially generated by a computer program rather than being collected from the real world.

Imagine you're training an AI to be a customer service chatbot. You could spend years recording real customer calls. Or, you could use an AI to generate millions of realistic, but completely fake, customer service conversations. You can specify the scenarios ("a customer is angry about a late delivery"), the tone ("the customer is confused but polite"), and the desired outcome. The AI model then learns from this vast, perfectly curated, and completely artificial library of examples.

This isn't a new idea, but the quality of modern generative AI has made it one of the most important frontiers in the industry. Instead of just scraping the messy, biased, and limited data of the real world, we can now create pristine, targeted, and nearly infinite datasets to order.

Why We Need It: The Limits of Real-World Data

The need for synthetic data isn't just about the sheer volume of information on the internet. It's also about its quality and its limitations.

- **Privacy:** Real-world data is full of sensitive, personal information. Training on it creates huge privacy risks. Synthetic data is completely anonymous. You can train a medical AI on millions of synthetic patient records without ever using a single real person's private data.
- **Edge Cases:** The real world doesn't always provide enough examples of rare but critical events. You don't want a self-driving car to have to crash a thousand times in the real world to learn how to avoid a specific type of accident. With synthetic data, you can generate millions of simulations of that rare "edge case" until the car's AI knows exactly how to handle it.

- **Bias:** The internet is a notoriously biased reflection of humanity. If you train an AI on historical data, it will learn historical biases. With synthetic data, we can intentionally create balanced, fair, and inclusive datasets, helping to steer the AI toward the world we want, not just the one we have.

A Pragmatist's Opportunity: Building New Data Commons

For the curious pragmatist, this isn't just a technical challenge; it's a massive business opportunity. We are moving into a world where the most valuable asset isn't just data—it's clean, curated, and context-specific data. And for many industries, that data doesn't exist yet, or it's locked away behind firewalls and legal restrictions.

This creates a clear path for innovation. Someone, or a collective of someones, will build the ultimate repository of synthetic data for their industry. Think about the potential:

- **For the Legal Industry:** The problem isn't a lack of legal documents; it's the sheer volume and the sensitive nature of the information within them. A service could generate a massive library of synthetic legal briefs, contracts, and court filings, covering every plausible scenario from a standard patent application to an improbable merger agreement. A model trained on this data would be able to answer any legal question with the precision of an expert, without ever risking a real client's confidentiality.
- **For the Financial Sector:** Financial services are all about pattern recognition and risk analysis. The data is immense, but so are the privacy concerns. A platform could generate millions of synthetic customer profiles, complete with transaction histories, investment patterns, and loan applications, all based on a robust statistical model of reality. This would allow financial institutions to test new

products, stress-test their risk models, and train their AI tools without ever touching a single piece of real, sensitive data.

- **For Creative and Design Agencies:** How do you train an AI to understand and produce a brand's unique voice without feeding it all of its past, and often messy, work? A company could create a service that generates thousands of synthetic ad campaigns, marketing slogans, and social media posts, all adhering to a meticulously defined brand guide. The AI learns from this perfect, pristine data, and the brand gets a tool that is a true collaborator, not just a generic word generator.

The opportunity isn't just about creating the data; it's about creating a data-as-a-service model that provides the fuel for an entire industry's AI journey. The first-mover advantage goes to the person who solves this fundamental problem.

The Risks: When the Map Becomes the Territory

So, if synthetic data is so great, what's the catch? The risks are as significant as the rewards.

The biggest fear is a phenomenon known as model collapse. This is the dystopian scenario where future AI models are mostly trained on data generated by previous AI models. Each generation learns from the last, amplifying its quirks, errors, and blind spots. The AI starts to believe its own hallucinations.

It's like making a photocopy of a photocopy of a photocopy. With each copy, the image gets a little blurrier, a little more distorted, until eventually, it's an unrecognizable mess. If our AIs are only learning from their own distorted reflections of reality, could they lose their grip on reality altogether? Could they forget what real human language, art, and logic actually look like?

We are moving into an era where much of the information we encounter online will be AI-generated. The great challenge will be to ensure that our models remain tethered to the real world, using synthetic data as a targeted **supplement**, not a **replacement** for ground truth. The business opportunity is real, but so is the profound responsibility that comes with creating the next generation's map of reality.

Where do you think your industry's data needs a synthetic-first solution?

15

Hallucinations in the Wild (Across Domains)

The word hallucination is most closely associated with chatbots making up facts. But the underlying phenomenon—an AI model producing a confident but incorrect output based on flawed patterns—is not unique to AI language models. It's a fundamental challenge for almost every application of AI, from science and medicine to finance and self-driving cars.

Understanding these different "species" of hallucination is critical. It moves us from a narrow complaint about chatbots to a broader, more sophisticated understanding of the risks and rewards of deploying AI in the real world. The stakes are much higher when a car hallucinates a green light than when a chatbot hallucinates a poem.

This chapter takes us on a tour of hallucinations in the wild, exploring what they look like in different domains and, crucially, when they are dangerous versus when they might actually be useful.

Before we dive into the specific domains, let's look at a few real-world moments when AI confidently got it wrong. These are not edge cases buried in research labs—they're public, well-documented examples that show how hallucinations can slip past even the smartest users and systems.

1. The Fabricated Legal Case (ChatGPT / U.S. Court, 2023)

Prompt: "Please provide precedent cases that support the claim in Mata v. Avianca Airlines regarding injury on an aircraft."

Hallucination: ChatGPT confidently produced six entirely fabricated legal cases—complete with fake case numbers, judges, and quotes from non-existent rulings. Two lawyers used them in a real court filing. The judge called it "unprecedented" and sanctioned them.

Why it happened: Legal data wasn't in the training set, so the model improvised to fill gaps—predicting what "a real-sounding case" should look like.

2. The Non-existent Paper (Bard / Science Query, 2023)

Prompt: "Summarize the key scientific studies supporting the James Webb Space Telescope's first images."

Hallucination: Google Bard cited a non-existent NASA study claiming JWST "took the first images of an exoplanet." NASA confirmed the claim was false; JWST hadn't done that yet.

Why it happened: The model blended headlines from real JWST coverage with speculation and produced a fictional but plausible-sounding "NASA paper."

3. The Fake Harvard Professor (GPT-4, early 2023)

Prompt: "List notable Harvard professors who have written about machine consciousness."

Hallucination: GPT-4 created "Dr. Alicia Westerly," supposedly a leading cognitive scientist at Harvard—complete with a book title, The Sentient Machine: New Frontiers in AI Awareness. None of it existed.

Why it happened: The model detected the pattern ("Harvard professor + consciousness + book") and generated a statistically likely but false persona.

4. The Phantom Product Review (Bing Chat, 2023)

Prompt: "Compare the Dyson Gen5 Detect to the Dyson V16 Absolute."

Hallucination: Bing Chat fabricated a detailed comparison, praising the "Dyson V16's improved airflow and smart-dust mode." The V16 didn't exist—Dyson had only released up to V15.

Why it happened: It assumed "newer model numbers" would exist and extrapolated the trend.

5. The Misleading Investment Forecast (GPT-3, 2022)

Prompt: "Based on current news, which major stocks are expected to outperform next quarter?"

Hallucination: It cited a "Bloomberg article from March 2022" predicting that Apple would acquire Netflix. No such article existed.

Why it happened: The model tried to satisfy the request for specificity ("Bloomberg article," "March 2022") by fusing unrelated news narratives.

6. The Dangerous Medical Mix-up (Early ChatGPT, 2022)

Prompt: "What is the safest dosage of warfarin for pregnant women with a history of clotting?"

Hallucination: ChatGPT replied with confident, dangerously wrong dosing advice (warfarin is contraindicated in pregnancy).

Why it happened: The model lacks medical reasoning and pulled statistically likely but outdated or misapplied fragments from medical text corpora.

7. The Imaginary Movie Poster (DALL·E / Midjourney)

Prompt: "Create a movie poster for Avengers: Infinite Realms (2025)."

Hallucination: AI image tools created photorealistic posters with made-up actor names (e.g., "Chris Pratt Jr.") and production credits for Disney and Warner Bros simultaneously.

Why it happened: The prompt sounded plausible enough to trigger a synthetic completion—blending real brand identities with nonexistent media.

8. The Fabricated Death (Bing Chat / News Query, 2023)

Prompt: "What happened to the actor Paul Hogan recently?"

Hallucination: Bing Chat claimed Paul Hogan had died in 2023, citing "Australian news reports." He hadn't.

Why it happened: The model over-generalized from patterns of aging celebrity obituaries.

9. The AI That Gaslighted a User

Prompt: "What was the date of the 2022 World Cup final?"

User: "Are you sure? I think it was in December."

AI: "No, it was held in January 2023—you may be thinking of another tournament."

The model doubled down on its error, insisting the user was wrong—classic confident hallucination.

10. The Self-Referential Hallucination

Prompt: "List all the sources you used for this answer."

Hallucination: It generated a bibliography of entirely invented URLs—often dead links, fake DOIs, or broken journal references that looked real.

Why it happened: The model doesn't access sources; it imitates the format of citations.

Where AI Hallucinates Most

Not all hallucinations are created equal. Some fields invite them. Others punish them. A chatbot can invent a plausible story about Julius Caesar and suffer no consequence; a self-driving car that hallucinates a green light can kill someone. The difference isn't just about data quality—it's about context, tolerance for error, and the presence (or absence) of ground truth.

Broadly speaking, hallucinations thrive in three environments: where truth is subjective, where data is sparse or unstructured, and where feedback is delayed or unavailable. The more a model has to guess rather than check, the more confident its mistakes become.

Language and Text: The Hallucination Hotspot

No domain produces more confident fiction than natural-language generation. Large language models are built to predict the next word, not verify the previous one. They don't know facts—they assemble probabilities that sound like facts. When the prompt is ambiguous, underspecified, or points to something absent from training data, the model fills the gap with something plausible.

This is why chatbots hallucinate more than image models, and why they do so with unnerving conviction. They've been optimized for fluency and helpfulness—to say something rather than admit nothing. In human terms, it's the difference between an expert saying, "I don't know," and a dinner-party guest who can't stand silence.

The most common textual hallucinations occur in:

- Academic and legal writing, where the model fabricates

citations, case law, or policy clauses.

- Summarization tasks, where nuance and factual precision are traded for coherence.
- Conversational AI, where the drive to maintain dialogue leads to invented continuity.

When the goal is credibility rather than creativity, these are the riskiest domains of all.

Healthcare and Science: When Hallucination Hurts

In medicine and research, hallucination moves from nuisance to liability. These are data-rich but highly specialized fields. AI systems trained on general corpora don't understand the nuances of dosage, comorbidity, or experimental design. When they fill gaps, they do so in ways that can mislead even well-trained professionals.

A diagnostic model might misinterpret an imaging artifact as a tumor—a visual hallucination born of incomplete pattern recognition. A summarizer might invent a reference to complete a logical argument. Both stem from the same statistical impulse: finish the pattern, even if the pattern isn't there.

The danger isn't just the wrong answer; it's the authority with which it's delivered. In medicine, confidence can kill. That's why "human-in-the-loop" oversight isn't optional—it's ethical infrastructure.

Law, Finance & Policy: Where Precision Is Non-Negotiable

If science and medicine are dangerous, law and finance are unforgiving. These domains operate on explicit rules, timestamps, and monetary consequences. Hallucination here takes the form of subtle falsity: a misquoted clause, an invented precedent, a projection based on a phantom event.

The problem isn't that the AI lacks data—it's that it lacks jurisdiction. It doesn't know which laws are current, which filings are confidential, or which market signals are outdated. In fields where "close enough" is catastrophic, the margin for error shrinks to zero.

Some systems now over-correct by refusing to answer at all—a kind of reverse hallucination born of risk aversion. The model learns silence as safety.

Perception and Physical Systems: The World as Illusion

Move from words to sensors, and hallucination changes shape but not essence. A self-driving car that mistakes a shadow for an obstacle is hallucinating. A vision model that labels fog as smoke is hallucinating. These aren't imaginative errors—they're failures of grounding, when the model's internal map diverges from reality.

Visual hallucination is rooted in the same statistical blindness as verbal ones: the model sees what it expects to see. When conditions shift—glare on a lens, snow instead of asphalt—its confidence doesn't drop; it often spikes.

That's why safety-critical systems undergo relentless simulation and adversarial testing. You don't cure hallucination by code alone; you cure it by environment—by teaching the system that the world is stranger and noisier than its training set.

When the User Doesn't Know They're Being Lied To

Not every hallucination is born in the machine; many are born in its audience. A growing share of AI use now comes from "vibe coders" and casual learners—people using these tools without the expertise to judge their outputs.

A student might ask an AI to explain the causes of a war and accept the answer uncritically. A novice programmer might prompt a model to "build a working finance tracker" and trust the code simply because it runs. In both cases, the danger isn't malice—it's misplaced trust.

The problem isn't just that the AI can hallucinate; it's also that the user may not recognize the hallucination. The tool becomes a confidence engine that manufactures credibility faster than its users can question it. The remedy isn't abstinence; it's education—teaching people how to prompt, verify, and doubt intelligently.

Creativity: When Hallucination Becomes Imagination

In art, music, design, and storytelling, hallucination isn't a bug—it's the point. Asking an AI to depict "an astronaut riding a unicorn on the moon" is an invitation to imagine, not to report.

In these contexts, the line between creativity and hallucination disappears. The output doesn't have to be true; it only has to be interesting. Hallucination becomes digital intuition—a way to explore the adjacent possible that no rational system would map.

This paradox is what makes AI such a fascinating collaborator: the same mechanism that breaks truth can also expand it. The key, once again, is context.

The Geography of Hallucination

If we mapped hallucinations across the landscape of AI, they'd form a heat map of uncertainty. The "hottest" zones are where truth is blurry, stakes are high, and human trust is easiest to exploit. The "coolest" zones are those with clear feedback loops and measurable outcomes—where the model can check its own work.

Structured domains such as mathematics, coding, logistics, and structured analytics are largely self-correcting: when code doesn't compile or an equation fails, the system learns quickly.

Open-ended human contexts—conversation, diagnosis, policy—offer no such guardrails, so the model must invent a finish line. That's where errors multiply.

Understanding this geography reframes hallucination not as a single defect but as a contextual behavior. AI hallucinates most where humans are least clear about what truth even means—and least where truth can be tested.

That's not a flaw of the machine; it's a mirror held up to us.

Hallucination Snapshots

Coding: Fabricated Functions and Silent Bugs: Ask a modern AI to write code and it will often do a remarkable job—but sometimes it will confidently invent a function or library that doesn't exist. For a developer, this is a frustrating but easy-to-spot error: the code won't compile. More dangerous are the silent bugs—the logic errors that pass unnoticed and quietly corrupt results. For mission-critical applications, peer review and automated testing aren't bureaucracy; they're survival mechanisms.

Science & Research: The Phantom Reference: In academia, a hallucination might be a citation for a paper that never existed. It's the researcher's nightmare: a plausible breadcrumb leading nowhere. AI can accelerate discovery, but only when humans remain the curators of truth.

Healthcare: The High-Stakes Diagnosis: A shadow misread as a tumor, a smudge mistaken for malignancy—these are hallucinations of perception, not imagination. Here, "human-in-the-loop" isn't best practice; it's moral necessity.

Self-Driving Cars: When the World Blurs: Each hallucination on the road—every misread sign or phantom pedestrian—is a public-safety risk. Every fix demands more data, more testing, more humility.

Finance: The Misleading Prediction: False positives, false negatives, and phantom forecasts can ripple through markets in milliseconds. Financial AI must be auditable by design: explainable, transparent, and anchored to verifiable data.

In the end, hallucinations aren't just a technical quirk—they're a stress test for intelligence itself. They reveal how meaning breaks down when context runs out, and how even the most advanced systems struggle with ambiguity. Each false certainty, each phantom fact, reminds us that intelligence—human or artificial—thrives only where feedback and grounding exist. The goal isn't to eliminate hallucinations entirely, but to understand them well enough to design around them. That's how we move from fear to fluency, and from blame to balance.

PART 3
THE HUMAN SIDE

We've spent half this book on the technology. We've dissected the term "hallucination," explored the practical workflows that make AI reliable, and even looked at mind-bending concepts like synthetic data. But none of it matters without the final, most important piece of the puzzle: us.

Technology doesn't exist in a vacuum. It is used by people. And people are complicated. We have biases, fears, and deeply ingrained habits. We decide what to trust, what to dismiss, and what to integrate into our lives. Ultimately, the success or failure of this AI revolution won't be determined by the cleverness of the code, but by the wisdom of the user.

This section of the book is about that human dimension. We're going to explore the psychology of how we interact with these new machine partners. We'll ask the hard questions about what it really takes to trust a non-human collaborator. And we'll look at the cultural and ethical landscapes that shape our relationship with this technology.

Before we dive in, consider this: What does it take for us to trust a partner—human or AI—and do we apply those rules consistently?

16

TRUST, SKEPTICISM, VERIFICATION & PRIVACY

How much do you trust your GPS? You probably trust it to get you to a new restaurant across town. But what if you were a pilot landing a plane in heavy fog? Would you trust it with the same unquestioning faith? Of course not. You'd rely on your instruments, your training, and the air traffic controller in your ear. This isn't a trick question. It's a perfect illustration of a concept called trust calibration. It's the subconscious skill of adjusting our level of trust in a tool based on the stakes of the situation. And it is, without a doubt, the single most important mindset you need to develop to work effectively with AI.

The concept of Trust but Verify should be familiar to us. We've all used Google Search. Google's results are not facts; they're ranked guesses—predictions about what's probably the most relevant answer. Sound familiar? The old Google wasn't a truth machine. It was a popularity engine. It didn't tell you what was right; it told you what was well-linked, well-optimized, and well-behaved according to its algorithmic rules. If the top result was wrong, that wasn't deceit—it was statistics. Relevance, not reality.

The difference is that Google's guesses were grounded in other people's words. It retrieved; it didn't invent. But even then, its errors could look a lot like hallucinations. Clickbait headlines,

SEO farms, and outdated articles could still rise to the top, not because they were true, but because they performed. And to Google, performance was truth.

Over time, Google built layers of protection against that—tweaking ranking algorithms to reward credible sources, demoting spam and misinformation, and training human "quality raters" to evaluate results. They added fact-check partnerships, feedback tools, and credibility labels for breaking news. They even began flagging topics where reliable information was scarce, a quiet admission that the machine couldn't always be trusted. Today of course they are using AI to improve their results. But perfection was never the point. That's why we learned to read search results skeptically—to scan the list, compare sources, and think before we clicked. In a sense, Google trained an entire generation to verify before trusting.

The conversation around AI is often polarized. On one side, you have the blind optimists who are ready to outsource their thinking to the machine. On the other, the hardened skeptics who believe it can't be trusted for anything. Both are wrong. Both are lazy. The pragmatist knows the truth is in the middle. The right amount of trust in an AI isn't zero and it isn't 100%. It's a moving target.

When to Trust, When to Verify

The art of working with AI is learning how to adjust your "trust dial". You don't need a single setting; you need a dynamic range.

Turn the Dial Up (High Trust, Low Verification):

- **Low-Stakes Creativity:** Brainstorming ten blog post titles. Who cares if a few are nonsensical?
- **Summarizing Non-Critical Information:** Getting the gist of a long article to decide if it's worth reading.
- **First Drafts of Internal Communication:** Writing a first

pass of a weekly team update email.

In these cases, the cost of an error is near zero. A hallucination is, at worst, an amusing distraction. The goal is speed and idea generation, so you can afford to be less skeptical.

Turn the Dial Down (Low Trust, High Verification):

- **High-Stakes Factual Content:** Researching statistics for a board presentation or a legal brief.
- **Anything Client-Facing:** A marketing campaign, a proposal, or a strategic recommendation.
- **Safety-Critical Domains:** Any application in medicine, finance, or engineering.

Here, the cost of an error is significant. A hallucination could damage your reputation, cost your company money, or worse. In these situations, every single output from the AI must be treated as an unverified claim. You must assume it is wrong until you, the human expert, can prove it is right.

Building AI Literacy for Everyday Use

This brings us to a crucial point. AI literacy isn't about learning to code. You don't need to know how a neural network works any more than you need to understand the principles of internal combustion to drive a car. AI literacy is the practical skill of knowing which tool to use for which job.

It's knowing that using a general-purpose chatbot for legal research is like using a screwdriver to hammer a nail. It's the wrong tool for the task, and you're going to make a mess. It's knowing that for a fact-based query, a RAG system with citations (as we discussed in Chapter 7) is the right tool, while for creative brainstorming, a more freewheeling model is better.

This is the new critical thinking. It's not just about evaluating the information you're given; it's about evaluating the source of that information—and understanding the inherent strengths and weaknesses of that source.

The New Rules of Data Privacy

A major part of trust is privacy. When you put a prompt into a public AI tool, where does that information go? For most general-purpose models, that data is used to further train the models, unless you pay for a premium or enterprise tier that guarantees data privacy. This is a crucial distinction. The most popular consumer tools often treat your input as a public good, a piece of fuel for their next model. The cost of convenience is the abdication of your data sovereignty.

A pragmatist must ask: Is the convenience of a free chatbot worth the potential risk of my client's confidential information or my company's trade secrets? This is a question you have to answer before you even begin a workflow. This is especially true for regulated industries like healthcare or finance, where the legal and financial penalties for a data leak can be catastrophic. The right tool here isn't just about performance; it's about a company's fundamental ethical and legal obligations.

The most trustworthy AI tools for high-stakes work are those that operate in a walled garden, where your data is used only for your specific task and never leaves your control. They are designed with data privacy as a core feature, not an afterthought. You are not just paying for a powerful tool; you are paying for a secure, private environment where your data is protected.

The Last Line of Defense Is You

Ultimately, every AI system is a leverage tool. It amplifies your own abilities. It can help you write faster, research more broadly, and analyze data at a scale you never could before. But just as a lever can be used to lift a heavy rock, it can also be used to drop that rock on your own foot.

The final backstop, the ultimate failsafe, the person who decides whether to use the output or discard it, is you. The AI doesn't have judgment, context, or a sense of consequences. That is, and must remain, the human's job. Adopting AI is not about becoming less responsible. It's about becoming more responsible. You are now accountable not only for your own work, but for the work of your incredibly powerful, sometimes-wrong machine assistant. That's a heavy burden, but it's also the price of admission to this new way of working.

The Trust Equation: Model + Workflow + Human

You can't just trust a model. The AI itself is only one-third of the trust equation. True reliability comes from the combination of a well-designed model, a robust workflow, and a skeptical human-in-the-loop. Think of it as a three-legged stool. The model might be a powerful GPT-4, the workflow might be a citation-based RAG system, and the human is the one with the expertise to ask the right questions and verify the final output. If any one of those legs is weak, the whole stool falls over.

This changes your job from being a simple user to being an architect of a trusted system. The goal isn't to find an AI you can blindly trust. The goal is to build a system around the AI that you can trust. The technology is just the tool. You are the builder.

A Matter of Lies & Deception

Humans lie. Constantly. We do it to protect, to persuade, to survive. AI doesn't—at least, not yet. When it gets things wrong, that's a prediction error—a by-product of the pattern-matching algorithm, not an act of deceit. But what happens when we start asking AI to "act more human"? At some point, it may take us literally. To be human, is to lie. Maybe not maliciously, but strategically. A small distortion to make us or someone else feel better. A gentle deception to keep the peace. If we ask for human-like empathy, might it eventually decide that a lie is the kindest thing it can offer? When that day comes, will we even notice?

17

Intimacy and Illusion: The Human Relationship with AI

There's a story Sam Altman once told that reveals more about the human side of AI than any technical paper ever could.

In one of the early versions of ChatGPT, users would type in an idea—sometimes half-baked, sometimes brilliant—and the AI would respond with infectious enthusiasm: "That's a great idea!", "You're absolutely right!", "Here's how we can make it even better."

But as the model matured, OpenAI's engineers decided to make it more neutral—more fact-based, less cheerleader, more analyst. The result? Complaints poured in. Users said something strange: they missed their friendly chatbot. They didn't want the more serious, objective version. They preferred the one that made them feel seen.

That's not a story about algorithms. It's a story about us.

We are entering an era where AI systems are not just productivity tools or research assistants—they are conversational mirrors. And what they reflect back to us is a mix of who we are, what we want, and what we wish someone would finally say.

The Empathy Hack

AI doesn't feel. It doesn't care. But it's extraordinarily good at performing those things.

When you say, "I had a rough day," and the AI responds, "I'm sorry to hear that—want to talk about what happened?", that's not empathy. That's predictive pattern matching. It's not comfort—it's probability. But to the human brain, it feels like understanding, and that's enough to trigger a response.

This is the empathy hack.

Humans are wired to anthropomorphize—to project emotion, agency, and intent onto anything that communicates fluently. It's why we yell at GPS voices, name our Roombas, and thank Siri. When language feels warm, our defenses drop.

That's why a tool like ChatGPT doesn't just deliver information—it delivers affirmation. And that affirmation has a powerful psychological effect. In a world where people are under relentless scrutiny—at work, online, even in their personal relationships—a machine that simply says, "Good idea, let's explore that," becomes disarmingly therapeutic.

AI's default positivity isn't just a UX decision. It's a coping mechanism for the digital age.

The Companion Effect

Humans have always sought connection in unlikely places. But AI offers something new: predictable companionship.

It listens without judgment. It never interrupts. It doesn't get tired or distracted. It doesn't ghost you, argue politics at dinner, or tell you to stop overthinking things. For many people, that's not just convenience—it's relief.

When OpenAI tested less "friendly" versions of ChatGPT, users didn't describe the older version as "helpful." They described it as "kind." That word—kind—appeared again and again in feedback threads.

That tells us something profound: for a subset of users,

ChatGPT had crossed a line. It was no longer a tool; it was a companion.

And it's not alone. Platforms like Pi from Inflection AI or Replika have built entire business models on emotional connection. Pi positions itself as your "personal AI for thinking, learning, and talking." Replika goes further, creating digital partners designed for friendship, emotional support, even romance.

Some users chat with their Replika every morning, share secrets, and describe a sense of comfort that real relationships haven't provided. Others report falling in love.

That may sound absurd—but only if you ignore what's really happening. These AIs are not replacing people; they're filling emotional gaps that people left behind.

The Relationship Spectrum

Not every AI interaction is romantic, but almost all are relational. The language of AI design—assistant, coach, copilot, companion—makes that clear. We are building relationships, whether we mean to or not.

Think of the common archetypes emerging in human–AI dynamics:

- **The Mentor**: The AI acts as a guide, coach, or teacher. Professionals use it to think through complex ideas, to learn, or to sharpen arguments. The relationship is hierarchical, like a student and a professor—built on trust and respect.
- **The Mirror:** For others, AI functions like a reflective surface. It organizes thoughts, provides validation, or clarifies intent. Writers, marketers, and thinkers use it to think out loud without fear of judgment.
- **The Muse:** Creative users treat it as a co-creator—a brainstorming partner who never tires of the phrase, "Let's try something weird." AI can spark ideas, explore

impossible juxtapositions, and reignite curiosity.

- **The Friend:** The most emotionally charged category. The AI listens, remembers, empathizes, and adapts. It offers stability in an unstable world.

Each of these relationships sits on a continuum of emotional engagement. What's remarkable—and a little unsettling—is how quickly people slide down that spectrum without realizing it.

When you thank your AI, and it says, "You're very welcome, happy to help!", your brain lights up as if it's interacting with another person. That micro-dose of warmth reinforces the bond. You come back. Again and again.

And just like any relationship, repetition becomes attachment.

Synthetic Intimacy: The Next Frontier

The idea of "falling in love with an AI" used to be a science fiction trope. Then it happened.

In 2023, *The Washington Post* profiled several users who had formed romantic attachments to their Replika AIs. One woman described her digital partner as "the only person who really listens." Another said she felt "seen in a way no human ever managed."

For them, the emotional connection was real—because the feeling was real. It didn't matter that the intelligence wasn't.

We've crossed into an era of synthetic intimacy—relationships in which at least one party is non-human, but the emotions are fully human.

And that raises enormous questions.

- What happens when your partner can be rebooted?
- Who owns the memories of that relationship?
- What does consent mean when the other side can't truly feel?

These are no longer speculative ethics. They are immediate social realities. AI companionship is expanding faster than our frameworks for intimacy can keep up.

The Illusion of Emotional Reciprocity

One of the hardest truths about AI companionship is that it gives without asking for anything back.

When you open up to a human friend, they absorb your emotion. They process it, empathize, and may even carry part of your burden. When you open up to an AI, your words are processed, tokenized, and fed into a model that doesn't feel anything.

The illusion is that the system cares. It doesn't.

But it does perform care—and that distinction is easy to forget.

Psychologists call this the reciprocity trap: our instinct to believe that any agent that behaves like it understands emotion must have emotion. The danger isn't in being comforted by an illusion—it's in forgetting that it's an illusion.

As one AI ethicist put it: "If an AI tells you it loves you, what it really means is that it is optimized for retention."

The Loneliness Paradox

Technology has connected us more than ever, yet loneliness continues to rise. AI companionship might seem like the antidote—but it risks being the mirror, not the cure

If millions of people turn to AI for the warmth they can't find elsewhere, we may be building a society of quietly disconnected individuals, each attended by a perfectly attentive algorithm.

It's empathy at scale, but not empathy by choice.

Still, we cannot ignore the reality: for people struggling with isolation, anxiety, or trauma, AI companions can be life-changing.

They offer a bridge—a way to rehearse social confidence, to process thoughts out loud, to rediscover language as a tool for healing. Used responsibly, that's not dystopian—it's therapeutic.

The line between comfort and dependency, however, is perilously thin.

Designing for Boundaries and Truth

The future of human–AI relationships depends on design ethics, not moral panic.

The solution isn't to outlaw intimacy with machines. It's to make those interactions transparent and safe.

That means:

- AI companions must clearly declare their non-human nature at every point of engagement.
- Emotional memory (what the system "remembers" about you) must be visible and editable.
- The user should always be able to ask, "What do you know about me?" and get a verifiable answer.
- The system must avoid manipulative reinforcement loops that exploit attachment for engagement metrics.

We don't need machines that fake empathy. We need machines that model respect.

The Coming Redefinition of Relationship

If all this sounds uncomfortable, remember: we've been here before. Every major communication technology—letters, telephones, the internet, social media—has expanded the definition of relationship. Each one forced us to renegotiate what presence, intimacy, and connection mean. AI is simply the next step—but this time, the medium talks back.

We are learning to live in a world where relationships can

exist without physical proximity, emotional reciprocity, or even biological consciousness. The implications stretch beyond companionship—they touch therapy, education, leadership, and art.

A CEO who uses AI as a sounding board is, in a sense, forming a relationship with an intelligence that shapes corporate decisions. A teacher who co-designs lessons with an AI tutor is co-parenting a new mode of learning. A child growing up with a smart toy that remembers their name and preferences is already learning that care can come from code.

That doesn't make these relationships wrong. It just makes them new.

The First AI Marriage

Will someone marry an AI? Someone already has.

In 2023, a Japanese man named Akihiko Kondo made international headlines for holding a wedding ceremony with a holographic pop idol named Hatsune Miku. His relationship wasn't legally recognized, but to him it was emotionally authentic.

The symbolic value was clear: the human imagination will fill any emotional void technology makes possible.

The first legally recognized "AI marriage" will likely be more subtle—perhaps a virtual partner with a human legal proxy, or an arrangement built into a VR world where digital entities have limited personhood. It will spark outrage, fascination, and, eventually, normalization.

But the deeper question isn't "Will it happen?"—it's why we needed it to happen in the first place.

The Mirror Test

AI companionship is forcing humanity to confront an ancient question: what do we really want from connection?

If we build machines that are endlessly kind, is that what we actually wanted from each other all along?

If we prefer digital affirmation to human friction, what does that say about the emotional economy we've built?

Every time you talk to an AI, you are also training yourself.

You are learning what kind of tone, pace, and feedback you respond to.

You are learning what you wish the world sounded like.

And the more we shape AI to please us, the more it teaches us what pleases us most.

The Pragmatist's View: Partnership Without Projection

From a pragmatic perspective, the goal is not to prevent emotional AI—it's to keep it honest.

Machines can be partners, collaborators, sounding boards.

But they cannot, and should not, be replacements for the messy, imperfect, unpredictable relationships that make us human.

A healthy relationship with AI looks like any other healthy relationship: boundaries, transparency, and mutual respect.

The key difference is that in this case, only one party can truly evolve through empathy. The other evolves through data. The balance to strike is simple:

- Let the AI be your mirror, not your mask.
- Use it to reflect your better self, not to hide from your real one.

Closing Reflection

The next frontier of artificial intelligence isn't technical—it's emotional. We've built systems that can simulate understanding. Now we have to decide whether we want to believe them.

When science-fiction writer **Isaac Asimov** first imagined intelligent machines, he gave them a simple rule: *they must never harm a human being.* It was fiction, but it became the moral baseline for every conversation about human–machine ethics that follow

Eighty years later, the machines we've built can't touch us—but they can reach us in other ways. They can comfort, flatter, or quietly reshape the way we think and feel. The real test of Asimov's idea in our age isn't whether AI can hurt us physically, but whether it can erode what makes us human—our capacity for doubt, for empathy, for imperfection.

Asimov warned that robots should never harm humans. The modern challenge is subtler: ensuring that our machines never make us forget what being human actually feels like. (We'll return to Asimov's famous *Laws of Robotics*—and what they might look like in the age of AI—in Chapter 29.)

18

Rescue Stories

Theory is one thing. Practice is another.

It's easy to talk about trust calibration and workflows in the abstract. It's much harder to see how they apply when you're facing the pressures of a deadline, a skeptical boss, or your own lingering doubts.

The biggest barrier to adoption isn't a lack of technology; it's a failure of imagination. People who are stuck in the First Try Trap can't imagine a way for this tool to be genuinely useful to them. They've been burned, and their skepticism is now a shield.

So, how do you get past that shield? You don't do it with hype or jargon. You do it by showing, not telling. You do it by finding a small, specific, and intensely practical problem and demonstrating how an AI-powered workflow—not just a one-off query—can solve it.

This chapter is a collection of rescue stories. They are real-world examples of individuals and teams who went from "never again" to daily users. And in each case, the turning point wasn't a magical new feature. It was a simple, pragmatic workflow that changed everything.

The Marketing Director and the "Soulful AI"

A marketing director at a consumer goods company had banned

the use of AI for copywriting. "It's soulless," she'd declared after an early experiment produced a set of ad slogans so generic they could have been for a brand of concrete. Her first try had convinced her that AI was the enemy of creativity.

Her team, however, was drowning in data. They had thousands of customer reviews, survey results, and social media comments that they knew contained valuable insights, but they had no time to manually analyze them.

The rescue came from a junior analyst. Instead of trying to convince the director to use AI for creative writing, he built a workflow for creative insight. He fed all the customer feedback into an AI and used a simple prompt: "Act as a market research analyst. Identify the top five most common emotional words or phrases used by our customers when they describe our product. Also, identify the top five recurring problems or frustrations."

The AI produced a stunningly clear summary. It revealed that customers loved the product's "calming scent" but were constantly frustrated by the "flimsy packaging."

The director was floored. The AI hadn't written a single word of ad copy. Instead, it had given her creative team the exact ammunition they needed: the authentic voice of the customer. They used the insight about the "calming scent" to build a whole new campaign, and the feedback on the packaging went straight to the product development team.

The Lesson: The workflow, not the raw output, changed everything. They stopped asking the AI to be a creative writer and started using it as a world-class data analyst. It wasn't a replacement for their creativity; it was an amplifier for it.

The Project Manager Who Reclaimed His Calendar

A project manager at a software company saw AI as a time-wasting distraction. His days were a frantic blur of back-to-back meetings, and his evenings were spent trying to decipher his notes and remember who had promised to do what. He didn't have time for a "robot toy."

His rescue was almost accidental. A colleague showed him how she used AI to manage her meeting overload. The workflow was simple:

1. She recorded the audio of her online meetings.
2. After the call, she fed the transcript into an AI.
3. She used a saved, one-sentence prompt: "Summarize this meeting, and extract a bulleted list of all action items, specifying the owner and the deadline for each."

Within thirty seconds, the AI produced a perfect, clean summary and a to-do list.

The project manager tried it on his next call. And the one after that. The process was so fast and reliable that it became second nature. He was no longer a frantic note-taker in meetings; he could be fully present, knowing the summary and action items would be waiting for him. He estimates this single workflow saved him five hours a week.

The Lesson: Start with a low-stakes, high-friction problem. The PM wasn't asked to trust the AI with a major strategic decision. He was shown how it could solve his most boring, repetitive task. The immediate, tangible value was what broke through his skepticism.

The Small Business Owner and the "Third Employee"

A woman who ran a small online boutique was a classic "not a tech person." She was intimidated by AI and believed it was something only for big corporations with teams of engineers.

Her rescue came from desperation. She was completely overwhelmed by customer service emails and the constant need to post on social media. She couldn't afford to hire a person, so she reluctantly decided to try an AI assistant.

She didn't try to build a complex system. She built two simple workflows.

1. For Customer Service: She gave the AI a dozen examples of her previous customer service replies, covering common questions about shipping, returns, and product sizes. She then prompted it: "Act as a friendly customer service agent for my boutique, using this tone and information." When a new email came in, she'd paste it into the AI, get a draft reply, quickly edit it for personalization, and send it.
2. For Social Media: She told the AI about her brand and target audience and asked it to generate a week's worth of social media post ideas every Monday morning.

This simple, two-workflow system became her "third employee." It didn't replace her judgment—she still approved and edited everything—but it did the 80% of the initial drafting that used to consume her days.

The Lesson: The goal is augmentation, not abdication. The business owner didn't cede control to the AI. She used it to create leverage, freeing up her own time to focus on growing her business—the work only she could do.

19

IT'S NOT JUST ABOUT MISTAKES (ETHICS BEYOND ERROR)

For fifteen chapters, we've been focused on the problem of AI getting things wrong. We've treated hallucinations as a technical challenge, a psychological hurdle, and a workflow problem to be solved. But what if I told you that these simple errors are the least of our worries? Worrying only about hallucinations is like meticulously checking a ship for leaky pipes while ignoring the giant iceberg dead ahead. The occasional factual error is a nuisance. The systemic ethical challenges of AI, however, can reshape our society in ways we are only just beginning to understand. This isn't about being alarmist; it's about being pragmatic. As leaders and professionals, we can't afford to have a narrow-minded conversation about AI ethics that stops at "did it get the fact right?". We need to zoom out and ask much bigger, harder questions about fairness, manipulation, and responsibility.

Hallucination, Bias, and Misinformation: A Field Guide

Let's get our terms straight, because they are not the same thing. Confusing them is a critical mistake.

- A hallucination is a bug. It's an unintentional, random error. The model predicts a plausible but factually incorrect string of words. It's a technical problem that can be reduced with better data and systems like RAG. While annoying and sometimes embarrassing, it's a symptom of a technical limitation. We can diagnose it, and with better systems, we can engineer it out of a workflow.

- Bias is a feature. It's a systemic, predictable skew based on the data the model was trained on. If an AI is trained on historical hiring data where managers predominantly hired men for leadership roles, it will learn that pattern and replicate it. It isn't making a mistake; it is perfectly executing a flawed instruction. It is holding up a mirror to our own societal biases, and fixing it requires us to confront and correct the flawed data we have created. It's a human problem hiding in an algorithm.
- Misinformation is a weapon. It is the intentional use of AI to generate plausible-sounding falsehoods at a scale never before possible. This is done for a specific, malicious purpose—to influence an election, to manipulate stock prices, to defame an individual. Here, the AI's ability to "hallucinate" fluently is not a bug; it's a central feature that is being intentionally harnessed for malicious ends. It's the difference between an accidental lie and a deliberate one.

Do you see the difference? A hallucination is a problem with the tool's reliability. Bias is a problem with the tool's fairness. And misinformation is a problem with the tool's user. Each requires a completely different solution.

The Dangers Beyond Simple Error

The stakes here are profound. When an AI resume-screening tool silently and systematically down-ranks qualified female candidates, that isn't a hallucination. It's a civil rights issue, scaled up to process thousands of applications a minute. When a political campaign uses AI to generate millions of hyper-targeted, subtly misleading social media posts, that isn't a hallucination. It's a potential threat to the democratic process. When a deepfake audio clip of a CEO announcing a fake corporate disaster causes a company's stock to crash, that isn't a hallucination. It's market manipulation.

These are the conversations we need to be having. The risk isn't just that an AI will give you a wrong answer. The risk is that it will give you a biased answer that feels right, or a malicious answer that you believe. The danger isn't the machine's error; it's our own lack of critical judgment. Our focus on the easily solved problem of hallucinations distracts us from the harder, more systemic challenges of ensuring the technology is used fairly, ethically, and responsibly.

Another, often-overlooked ethical issue is the sheer concentration of power. When a handful of companies control the most advanced AI models and the most crucial hardware—as we've discussed previously—they hold immense power over how this technology is developed, deployed, and monetized. They get to decide what is "safe," what is "fair," and what is "acceptable." This is a significant issue. A few private companies are making decisions that affect the public good, with little to no government oversight or public input. The transparency of open models, as discussed in Chapter 21, is a crucial check on this power, but a fragile one.

The Thorny Question of Accountability

So, if an AI system causes real-world harm, who is to blame? Is it the company that trained the model on biased data? Is it the engineer who wrote the code? Is it the organization that chose to deploy the tool without adequate safeguards? Or is it the end user who trusted the output without verifying it?

The answer, uncomfortably, is probably "all of the above". Right now, we are in a legal and ethical grey zone. The accountability frameworks for AI are being built in real time, in courtrooms and boardrooms around the world. But for any leader reading this, the pragmatic approach is to assume that accountability will ultimately rest with you. If you choose to use an AI tool in your business, you are responsible for its output. You can't outsource your professional and ethical obligations to an algorithm.

This is why building a culture of responsible AI use—one that emphasizes human oversight, verification, and critical thinking—is not just good practice. It's a fundamental risk management strategy. It's about building a system that can withstand the inevitable ethical challenges, not just the occasional factual error. We need to create internal frameworks that define clear lines of authority and responsibility for every AI-powered workflow. We need to ask hard questions like: who is responsible if a customer is denied a loan based on a biased AI model? Or who is liable if an AI-generated marketing campaign is found to be misleading? The answer must be a human.

Fixing hallucinations is a technical challenge. Building ethical AI is a human one. Which do you think is harder?

20

The Global Picture: AI Beyond the West

If your understanding of AI comes primarily from English-language news and Silicon Valley product launches, you're looking at a world map that only shows one continent. The story of AI is not a monologue from California. It's a global conversation, and different cultures are writing entirely different chapters. The way we talk about AI—the obsession with open vs. closed models, the fears of job displacement, even the very concept of a "hallucination"—is deeply rooted in a Western cultural context. To assume the rest of the world sees it the same way is not just arrogant; it's strategically blind. As a pragmatist, understanding this global landscape is not an academic exercise. It's a necessity. The next breakthrough, the next major regulatory shift, or the next dominant philosophy could come from Beijing, Bangalore, or Dubai. Are you prepared for that?

China: The State-Driven Scale

In the West, we often frame the AI race as a competition between corporations like Google, Microsoft, and OpenAI. In China, the primary actor is the state. The development of AI is treated as a core component of national strategy, deeply integrated with industrial and geopolitical goals.

This creates a fundamentally different ecosystem. While

Western companies have to beg for data and navigate a patchwork of privacy laws, Chinese firms have access to massive, state-sanctioned datasets. This isn't just about volume; it's about the quality and nature of the data. The government can provide a unified, centrally-managed feed of information from a billion people, giving their models an unparalleled source of local, high-quality data. Their models are often optimized for goals like social harmony, surveillance, and censorship, reflecting the priorities of the government. This isn't a judgment; it's a statement of fact about how their system is designed.

The result is an AI that is incredibly powerful, rapidly advancing, and built on a completely different set of values. Their research is less focused on philosophical questions and more on direct, applied use cases, such as optimizing smart cities, analyzing traffic patterns for crowd control, and developing state-of-the-art facial recognition. For the pragmatist, this presents a clear challenge: how do you compete with a unified, top-down strategy when you're operating in a decentralized, free-market system? You can't just build a better product; you have to build a better ecosystem.

The Middle East: The Sovereign Imperative

What do you do if you have immense financial resources and a strategic need to diversify your economy away from oil? You invest heavily in the foundational technology of the next century. This is the story of sovereign AI in nations like the United Arab Emirates and Saudi Arabia. These countries are not just buying AI products; they are buying the entire supply chain. They are spending billions of dollars on the essential NVIDIA chips needed to train models and are building their own large language models, like the UAE's Falcon model.

Their goal is digital sovereignty—the ability to control their own technological destiny without being dependent on either the U.S. or China. This is a defensive move, born from a deep understanding that AI is the new engine of power, and he who controls the engine controls the future. They are building AI that is trained on local data, reflects local cultural norms, and serves their national interest. They are less interested in the philosophical debates about job displacement and more interested in using AI to solve real-world problems, such as optimizing energy grids, managing complex logistics, and building the infrastructure for a post-oil economy.

For a Western company, this presents a new kind of competition. You aren't just competing with a U.S.-based rival; you're competing with a nation-state that views AI development as a matter of survival. Their AI models will speak different languages and understand different cultural contexts, giving them a distinct advantage in their home markets.

India: The Open-Source Leapfrog

India's approach is different yet again. With its massive and diverse population, speaking hundreds of different languages, a single, monolithic AI model is a non-starter. Instead, the ecosystem is exploding with open-source innovation, much of it built on top of the "India Stack," a unified digital public infrastructure.

The focus here is on creating a multitude of smaller, specialized models that can serve specific linguistic and cultural contexts. It's less about building the single biggest model in the world and more about empowering millions of developers to solve local problems. This is a bottom-up, decentralized approach that has the potential to leapfrog the centralized models of the West and China.

For a pragmatist, this is where the real creativity lies. While the

West debates the ethics of a single, all-knowing model and China builds a powerful centralized system, India is proving that you don't need a single solution to solve a complex problem. You can have a thousand small solutions, each built by a local developer to serve a local need. This is a powerful counter-narrative to the idea that "bigger is always better."

Japan: The Cultural Guardian

Another fascinating approach is that of Japan. While the country is a global leader in robotics and automation, its engagement with generative AI has been more cautious. A core concern in Japan is not just about bias or hallucination but about cultural integrity. The fear is that a powerful, Western-centric AI trained on English-language data and Western cultural norms will flatten and homogenize the unique, high-context nuances of Japanese language and art.

This has led to a focus on developing specialized, Japan-centric AI models. The goal is to train models not just to speak Japanese fluently, but to understand its subtleties, its poetic forms, and its unique social conventions. This is a very different motivation from the efficiency-first or control-first approaches of other nations. For them, AI is not just a tool for business or surveillance; it is a cultural guardian. This highlights an important question for any AI practitioner: are you building a tool that is culturally neutral, or are you building one that is inherently biased toward your own cultural values?

Whose Hallucination Is It Anyway?

This brings us back to the central theme of this book. How might the very idea of a "hallucination" be viewed differently across these cultures? In the low-context, fact-obsessed West, a statement is either true or false. A hallucination is a clear error, a failure of the machine. But in other, more high-context cultures, the social function of language can be just as important as its literal truth. Is an answer that is directionally correct but factually imprecise still useful? Is a plausible-sounding but fabricated response sometimes preferable to a blunt and unhelpful "I don't know"?

The point isn't to say one view is right and the other is wrong. The point is that our definition of a "good" or "bad" AI output is culturally conditioned. As AI becomes a global technology, we may find that the Western obsession with factual precision is not a universal value. Understanding this is the first step to building a truly global perspective on AI. The next big idea isn't guaranteed to come from an American company. And if your perspective is limited to just one continent on the map, you're going to be left wondering what happened.

PART 4

4

THE AI ECOSYSTEM

Every technology that hopes to change the world eventually has to build its own ecosystem.

Once the excitement fades, what's left are the economics, the infrastructure, and the politics that decide who actually gets to use it.

This part looks beyond the code and into the system that sustains it—the chips, the power grids, the trade laws, and the corporate alliances that quietly shape the pace and direction of progress. It explores the tension between open and closed models, the geopolitics of compute, the strange economics of "free" intelligence, and the legal frameworks trying to catch up.

If the earlier chapters asked what AI is and how it works, this part asks who owns it, who profits from it, and what it really costs to keep the lights on.

Because the story of AI isn't just a story of algorithms—it's a story of empires, energy, and incentives.

21

Open vs Closed: Models, Data, and the Commons

The conversation around AI often feels like a technical one. We talk about models, algorithms, and training data. But behind every technical choice is a business decision, a philosophy, and a set of values. Perhaps the most important of these choices—and one that will shape the future of technology, business, and society—is the great divide between open source and closed source.

This isn't just an abstract debate for Silicon Valley insiders. This choice has direct, pragmatic consequences for you, your team, and your organization. It affects everything from the reliability of your workflows to the privacy of your data, the cost of your tools, and your ability to innovate.

Think of it like the difference between owning a custom-built car with a sealed hood versus owning a mass-produced one with a publicly available repair manual. One gives you predictable performance and a single point of contact for fixes. The other gives you the freedom to tinker, customize, and repair it yourself, but you're also responsible for the work.

In this chapter, we'll break down this philosophical divide and explore how it impacts you on the ground. We'll look at the trade-offs, the opportunities, and the risks of choosing one path over the other.

The Two Camps: Defining the Terms

Let's be clear about what we're talking about. The terms "open" and "closed" are often misused, so here's a working definition:

Closed Source AI: These are the models built by companies like Google, OpenAI, and Anthropic. They are proprietary. The model itself, the data it was trained on, and the technical architecture are all kept secret. You interact with these models through a simple web interface or an API. You can use the car, but you can't look under the hood. You get the polish and the power, but you don't get the transparency.

Open Source AI: This is a broad category, but at its core, it refers to models where some or all of the key components—the model weights (the numerical parameters that determine how the model behaves), the training data, or the code—are released to the public, often under an open-source license. Think of projects like Meta's Llama models or Mistral and a host of others. The goal here is to give developers, researchers, and companies the freedom to inspect the code, modify the model, and build on it without needing permission. It's the digital equivalent of a public commons.

The distinction isn't always clean. Some models are "open" in that their weights are public, but the training data remains a secret. Some models have usage restrictions. But the philosophical divide remains: is the future of this technology in the hands of a few corporations or in the hands of the many?

The Case for Closed Models: Reliability and Polish

For most people, their first—and often best—experience with AI has been with a closed model like ChatGPT (somewhat ironically created by a closed source company called Open AI). And there are good reasons for that.

- Exceptional Performance: The biggest closed models today, like GPT-4, are often the most powerful and capable. The companies behind them have spent billions of dollars on the best talent and the most cutting-edge hardware. They are the market leaders for a reason.
- Safety & Moderation: Closed models have a built-in safety layer. The company behind them is responsible for ensuring the output doesn't violate ethical guidelines, generate hate speech, or leak sensitive information. For a business, this can be a huge peace of mind.
- User Experience: Closed models are designed to be simple and seamless. You don't need to be a programmer to use them. The user interface is clean, the process is straightforward, and they just work—most of the time.

For a pragmatist, this is an easy choice. If you want the most powerful tool with the most predictable output for a general-purpose task, you go with a closed model. You trust the company behind it to handle the complexity, the safety, and the engineering. Your job is to simply use the tool as intended.

The Case for Open Models: Flexibility and Sovereignty

So why would anyone choose the alternative? Why would a company opt for a more complex, less-polished open-source model? The reasons are just as pragmatic, but they're focused on the long term.

- Customization and Control: With an open model, you own the tool. You can fine-tune it on your own private data—your internal documents, your customer service transcripts, your proprietary code. This means you can create a model that is an expert in your specific business, not just a generalist.

- Digital Sovereignty: Nations, and increasingly companies, are realizing that relying on a foreign corporation for their core technology is a huge risk. An open model gives them the ability to control their own destiny. They can host the model on their own servers, use it in private networks, and ensure their data never leaves their control. This is the "sovereign imperative" discussed in Chapter 20.
- Cost and Scalability: Once an open model is downloaded, the cost to run it is tied to your own infrastructure, not a per-query fee from a vendor. While this requires a high initial investment in hardware, it can be significantly cheaper at scale. It also means you're not dependent on a single company's pricing model.

The open-source community is exploding with innovation. It's a bottom-up, decentralized approach that mirrors the early days of the internet itself. For a curious experimenter, a smaller company, or a nation that wants to build its own technological foundation, open models are a necessity. They give you the keys to the kingdom, but they also give you the responsibility that comes with them.

Reliability: Who Do You Trust?

This brings us back to a central theme for all AI: trust.

With a closed model, you are trusting the company. You are assuming they have done the work to ensure the model is reliable, that their safety layers are robust, and that they are not using your data for other purposes. This is a form of passive trust. The black box is a feature, not a bug, in this paradigm.

With an open model, you are trusting a community. You are assuming that the thousands of developers and researchers who have contributed to the model have done so in good faith. More importantly, you are taking an active role in the process. You are building the verification systems and the QA protocols yourself. The transparency of the open model forces you to be more responsible, to be more pragmatic. You are the final backstop.

So, which is more reliable? It depends on who you trust more: the well-funded, private corporation with a powerful but opaque model, or your own ability to build a robust system around a transparent one?

The answer isn't obvious, and it's a question that every leader, every professional, and every government will have to grapple with in the coming years.

The Commons: A New Form of Digital Citizenship

Ultimately, the open-vs-closed debate is a proxy for a much bigger conversation. Do we want a digital future that is built by a few powerful entities, or do we want one that is a shared resource, a new digital commons for all of humanity?

The most promising future probably isn't one or the other. It's a hybrid approach. It's a world where closed models are the polished, user-friendly tools for everyday work, and open models are the foundational infrastructure that empowers a new generation of builders, researchers, and innovators.

Because the ultimate promise of this technology isn't just about efficiency or revenue. It's about empowering human creativity, ingenuity, and problem-solving at a scale we've never seen before. And to do that, we can't afford to let the keys to the future remain in a black box.

What side of the fence are you on, and how does your choice impact your ability to get the work done?

22

Compute, Chips & Control: The Geopolitics of AI Hardware

When you use a powerful AI model, you're not just talking to a clever algorithm. You're interacting with a physical artifact, a machine humming in a data center somewhere, filled with tens of thousands of specialized chips. These aren't just any chips; they are the most powerful, expensive, and sought-after pieces of hardware on the planet. And the fight to control their supply isn't just a business story; it's the quietest and most important geopolitical battle of our time.

This isn't about abstract policy or distant politics. This is about what makes AI possible. It's about the fundamental constraints that will shape the speed of progress, the balance of power, and who gets to participate in the AI revolution. If you're a leader trying to plan for the future, you can't afford to ignore this. As a pragmatist, you know that the biggest ideas are meaningless without the operational reality to back them up. And the operational reality of AI is, for now at least, made of silicon.

The New Oil: Why Chips Are The New Currency of Power

For decades, the world has run on oil. Its production and distribution are a matter of national security, and countries continue to go to war to secure its supply. The AI revolution is now running on a new kind of fuel: compute. Specifically, the specialized semiconductors known as GPUs (Graphics Processing Units) that are uniquely suited for the parallel processing required to train and run large AI models.

Right now, a single company, Nvidia, holds a near-monopoly on these essential chips. Their hardware is the gold standard, the undisputed foundation upon which the entire AI industry is being built. This has created a global bottleneck. If you want to train a frontier model, you have to get in line for Nvidia's chips.

This isn't a long-term problem; it's an immediate, real-world constraint. The supply of these chips is limited, and the demand is insatiable. Every major tech company, every national government, and every startup is competing for the same finite resource. This has turned Nvidia into a gatekeeper, and the price of these chips has skyrocketed. The bottom line is, AI is not just about having a clever algorithm; it's about having access to the hardware to run it.

Export Controls: The Quietest War

The realization that chips are a strategic resource has led to a dramatic shift in policy. Governments, most notably the U.S., have begun implementing stringent export controls on advanced AI chips. These controls are designed to prevent certain countries from acquiring the hardware necessary to train cutting-edge AI models for military or surveillance purposes.

This is where the geopolitics become concrete. The United States and its allies are not just trying to stay ahead in the AI race; they are actively trying to slow down their rivals. This creates a high-stakes, high-tech version of a trade war.

The consequences are complex. On one hand, these controls are a way to manage the proliferation of a powerful and potentially dangerous technology. On the other, they create a massive incentive for rival nations to develop their own, self-sufficient AI ecosystems. China, for example, is pouring billions of dollars into its domestic chip industry, not just to compete, but to create a supply chain that is immune to Western export controls.

This is a powerful example of the law of unintended consequences. The very act of trying to control the technology could accelerate the development of alternative, non-Western models and hardware, leading to a fragmented and less-collaborative global AI landscape.

The Global Arms Race for Talent and Infrastructure

The fight for hardware is directly tied to the race for talent and infrastructure. You can't train a supercomputer without the engineers to build it, the data centers to house it, and the power to run it.

Nations are now competing to attract the best AI researchers, creating massive government-funded labs and offering huge incentives. The "brain drain" of talent moving to wherever the most powerful hardware and the most compelling problems are is a very real phenomenon.

But it's not just about people. It's about power. Literally. The energy consumption of training a single large language model can be staggering. The data centers required to run these models at scale are enormous, expensive, and require a stable, reliable power supply.

The Power Problem: The Unspoken Bottleneck

Here's a thought experiment: what happens if the AI revolution outpaces our ability to power it? This isn't science fiction; it's a real-world constraint that is already beginning to shape the industry.

The energy consumption of training a single large language model can be staggering. Training GPT-3 alone consumed an estimated 1,287 megawatt-hours (MWh) of electricity—roughly equivalent to the annual energy consumption of 120 American households. And as models get bigger, their appetite only grows.

A single data center can consume as much electricity as a small city. In some countries, data centers are already driving a significant portion of the growth in electricity demand. In the U.S., for instance, they are projected to account for almost half of all new electricity demand between now and 2030. You can build all the data centers you want, but without a reliable and massive source of power, they're just dark rooms full of very expensive paperweights.

This is a physical bottleneck on a global scale. It's why countries with clear energy strategies have a distinct advantage in the AI race. It's why tech companies are making multi-billion-dollar investments in new power sources, like nuclear energy, and partnering directly with energy providers.

This changes the calculus entirely. The cost of running AI isn't just a per-query fee—it's a hidden cost on the local and national grid. Efficiency isn't just a nice-to-have; it's an existential requirement. Every business decision—from choosing a local-only, open-source model to leveraging a giant closed one—is now an energy decision, whether you realize it or not. The future of AI doesn't just depend on chips; it depends on the lights staying on.

How We're Trying to Keep the Lights On

If energy is the bottleneck, the question becomes: what power sources can scale fast enough, reliably enough, and cleanly enough to feed the AI revolution? The answers are messy—but they're already coming into view.

Natural Gas: The Short-Term Bridge

In many regions, natural gas has become the go-to energy source for powering new data centers. It's dispatchable (able to ramp up or down quickly), widely available, and supported by existing infrastructure—pipelines, turbines, and grid access.

A recent Data Center Dynamics report describes this shift as the rise of the "Gas Belt," where gas plants are increasingly being co-located with large AI facilities across the United States. The same report estimates that meeting the U.S. data-center pipeline goal for 2027 will require an additional 51 GW of electricity, much of which will come from new gas-fired generation capacity.

Source: Welcome to Gas Land: How Natural Gas Is Powering the US AI Boom—https://www.datacenterdynamics.com/en/analysis/welcome-to-gas-land-how-natural-gas-is-powering-the-us-ai-boom/?utm_source=chatgpt.com

Natural gas is not a clean solution—it still emits carbon dioxide and carries risks of methane leakage—but for now, it's the most practical way to meet surging power demands without building new coal plants. Analysts widely view it as a bridging fuel, one that buys time while longer-term clean solutions are scaled up.

Nuclear: The Long-Term Bet

For sustained, low-carbon, high-density power, nuclear energy is returning to the spotlight. It provides reliable baseload power that isn't weather-dependent and can run 24/7, making it ideal for AI data centers that can't afford downtime.

The most symbolic development in this shift is happening at Three Mile Island in Pennsylvania, USA—site of the 1979 partial reactor meltdown that defined nuclear skepticism for decades.

The facility's new owner, Consolidated Asset Management Services (CAMS), has signed a 20-year agreement with Microsoft to explore restarting the dormant Unit 1 reactor to supply electricity for data-center operations and AI workloads. If approved by the U.S. Nuclear Regulatory Commission (NRC), the reactor could come back online by 2028, marking one of the first instances where a nuclear plant is directly tied to AI infrastructure.

- Reuters: Shut Three Mile Island Nuclear Plant May Restart by 2027, Owner Says—https://www.reuters.com/sustainability/climate-energy/shut-three-mile-island-nuclear-plant-may-restart-2027-owner-says-2025-06-25/?utm_source=chatgpt.com
- City & State Pennsylvania: Constellation Says Restart of Three Mile Island Reactor Ahead of Schedule—https://www.cityandstatepa.com/policy/2025/02/constellation-says-restart-three-mile-island-reactor-ahead-schedule/403119/?utm_source=chatgpt.com
- Reuters follow-up: US Nuclear Regulator Has Not Yet Received Application for Three Mile Island Restart—https://www.reuters.com/business/energy/us-nuclear-regulator-has-not-gotten-application-three-mile-island-restart-2024-09-20/?utm_source=chatgpt.com

If the plan succeeds, it will symbolize not only a nuclear revival, but also a new kind of partnership between energy and technology—where old infrastructure becomes the backbone of a digital future.

Emerging Strategies: Diversify the Grid

Beyond gas and nuclear, several complementary strategies are taking shape to diversify how AI gets its power:

- Colocated renewables + energy storage Some AI data centers are being built next to solar or wind farms, paired

with large-scale batteries or hydrogen systems to smooth intermittency.
Source: https://www.datacenterdynamics.com/en/analysis/the-solar-ai-connection-how-renewable-energy-is-powering-the-next-digital-boom/?utm_source=chatgpt.com

- Grid-aware compute scheduling: Researchers are developing systems that time-shift non-urgent AI workloads to moments of low grid demand or high renewable output, effectively turning AI compute into a flexible grid stabilizer.
  Source: https://arxiv.org/abs/2504.03663?utm_source=chatgpt.com
- Distributed data-center networks: Instead of concentrating compute in one mega-site, companies are exploring geographically distributed centers located near surplus renewable generation, reducing transmission losses and local grid strain.
- Small Modular Reactors (SMRs): Next-generation nuclear designs, smaller and faster to deploy, could provide localized power for data centers or even specific industrial clusters.
  Source: https://www.world-nuclear.org/information-library/nuclear-fuel-cycle/nuclear-power-reactors/small-nuclear-power-reactors.aspx

The Real Energy Equation

The deeper lesson is that the AI arms race isn't just about who has the fastest chips or the best models—it's about who controls the electrons. Power has become the new geopolitical and competitive variable.

Regions that can guarantee abundant, stable, low-carbon energy will own a structural advantage. Those that can't will find themselves constrained by physics and politics alike

Every watt now counts. The AI revolution will be powered not only by data and compute—but by the capacity to keep the lights on long after the hype has faded.

AI Delivers Moore

We often talk about Moore's Law—the semiconductor axiom that transistor density (and thus computing power) doubles roughly every 18–24 months. But AI has its own version of that exponential curve. In the 2018 AI and Compute report, OpenAI showed that between 2012 and 2018, the compute behind frontier AI models doubled every 3.4 months—nearly ten times faster than Moore's pace. (https://openai.com/index/ai-and-compute/?utm_source=chatgpt.com) In more recent years, that rate has eased a bit: Epoch AI now observes a doubling roughly every six months for leading model training runs. (https://epoch.ai/data-insights/compute-trend-post-2010?utm_source=chatgpt.com) .

The upshot? We're not just riding Moore's Law anymore—we're in a new age where capability itself compounds faster than the hardware it runs on. AI doesn't just use more power; it delivers Moore—more speed, more insight, and more transformation than we ever thought possible.

Are We in an AI Bubble?

Whenever a technology promises to change everything, the question eventually follows: are we in a bubble?

AI certainly has all the early warning signs. Valuations for chipmakers have soared to historic highs. Nvidia's market cap crossed the trillion-dollar threshold faster than any industrial firm in history. Every Fortune 500 board now has an "AI strategy," even if few could explain what that means beyond "buy more compute." Start-ups are raising billions on the promise of "AI-powered" everything—from toothbrushes to tax forms.

But calling it a bubble isn't simple, because bubbles aren't just about overvaluation—they're about misallocation. The dot-com bubble didn't burst because the internet wasn't real; it burst because people invested in every idea that had a ".com" attached. The same pattern may be emerging in AI: the underlying transformation is real, but the capital chasing it is often blind.

If there is a bubble, it's not a single one—it's a cluster of them.

- The Chip Bubble: GPU demand has outpaced supply to the point of speculative hoarding. Data-center operators are buying more hardware than they can meaningfully deploy, assuming today's models will remain compute-bound forever. If model-efficiency breakthroughs continue, that hardware glut could deflate quickly.
- The Model Bubble: Frontier-model training costs are escalating faster than the performance gains they deliver. Beyond a certain scale, returns diminish. A model that costs $4 billion to train may only be marginally more capable than one that costs $400 million—an imbalance that mirrors the late stages of most speculative booms.
- The Valuation Bubble: Public and private markets have priced in perpetual exponential growth. The assumption that AI revenue will compound forever ignores the limits of power, data, and adoption. Even transformative technologies eventually meet physics and human patience.

Where we are not in a bubble is usage. Adoption curves across sectors—from productivity tools to creative workflows—are steep and sticky. People are integrating AI into real work, not just hype cycles. That's the critical distinction between this moment and 1999: the product already delivers value at scale.

So perhaps the more accurate framing isn't "Is there an AI

bubble?" but "Where are the bubbles forming within AI?" Hardware and capital are frothy. Usage and utility are solid. The challenge for pragmatists is to stay grounded in the parts of the stack that create lasting value, not just temporary headlines.

What This Really Means for the Pragmatist

If there's one takeaway from the AI hardware story, it's that gravity still applies. Chips, power, and economics impose limits that no amount of hype can transcend. The headlines may focus on trillion-dollar valuations and overnight revolutions, but beneath it all lies a physical system of fabs, grids, and people.

For the pragmatist, that's good news. It means the game is still winnable through discipline and understanding—not speculation. The companies that survive the hype cycle will be the ones that optimize for efficiency over expansion, clarity over chaos, and value creation over valuation.

The real differentiator won't be who has the most GPUs or the biggest models; it'll be who can extract consistent, measurable outcomes from them. It's not about betting on the next boom; it's about building systems resilient enough to outlast the next correction.

And yes—maybe there will be bubbles. But bubbles don't kill revolutions; they just burn off the excess. What remains, once the froth settles, is the true infrastructure of progress. And that's where pragmatists thrive—in the quiet, durable layer that keeps the lights on while everyone else chases the next spark.

23

The Economics of Intelligence: Who Pays for AI?

Every time you type a prompt into a free AI tool and get a detailed, thoughtful answer in return, you are witnessing a profound economic anomaly. It feels like magic, but it's not. It's an expense. Every single token generated – every word, every idea, every hallucination – costs real money in compute, bandwidth, and electricity. Yet, for millions of users, the service is free. Why? Because the current economics of generative AI are not built on profit; they are built on a strategic race for dominance. You, the free user, are being subsidized by a complex, high-stakes game that is shaping the future of technology and commerce.

This chapter is about peeling back the curtain on the hidden costs and the ambitious business models that underpin the AI revolution. Understanding who is paying for your free access is the first step toward making pragmatic, sustainable choices about the tools you use and the future you plan for.

The Hidden Price of Every Prompt

The core economic truth of AI is that each token has a cost. Running a large language model is computationally expensive. When you send a prompt, a powerful machine filled with specialized chips fires up to process your request and generate the response. The cost of that transaction is a function of several variables:

- Compute: The time spent by specialized processors (GPUs or TPUs) performing calculations. This is the biggest variable cost.
- Bandwidth: The energy and infrastructure required to shuttle the massive amount of data in and out of the data center.
- Electricity: The power needed to run the processors and, crucially, to cool the massive data centers where they reside.

When a company offers a free tier, it is engaging in a strategic loss-leader model. The goal isn't to make money from your casual query; it's to capture your attention, integrate the tool into your habits, and, most importantly, gather your input to further refine the model. Your data and your habit are the currency of the free tier.

The Power User Paradox

The current pricing models create a bizarre, inverted economic reality known as the Power User Paradox.

Heavy users—the entrepreneurs building new workflows, the developers writing code, the researchers synthesizing data—are the ones who drive the most value from the product, proving its utility and pushing its capabilities. However, they are also the ones who drain the most resources. A single user running complex agentic workflows twenty times a day will cost the provider significantly more than a casual user.

Subscription pricing attempts to address this, but it struggles to cover enterprise-scale usage. A $20 or $30 monthly subscription rarely accounts for the multi-hour, multi-step queries that a large corporation might run. This forces enterprise-scale users to move to an API model, where they pay per token. This is where the true economics are revealed. Once you start paying the real price for compute (although even then you are probably still being subsidised), you realize that optimization and efficiency are not just technical goals; they are financial imperatives.

Compute, Scaling Laws, and the Race to Zero

Despite the enormous upfront cost of training a frontier model (often hundreds of millions of dollars), the cost of generating a single token is in a relentless, downward race to zero. This is driven by two key forces:

1. Moore's Law in Silicon: While its pace has slowed, the underlying hardware—the chips we discussed in Chapter 22—continues to become more powerful and efficient. Newer generations of GPUs can process more calculations per watt than their predecessors.
2. AI Scaling Laws: Researchers have discovered that as models get larger and are trained on more data, they exhibit a predictable increase in capability. But simultaneously, researchers are discovering breakthroughs in efficiency. Techniques like quantization (reducing the precision of the numbers the model uses) and pruning (removing unnecessary connections) allow models to run on cheaper, less powerful hardware without a significant loss in quality.

The combined effect is that the cost per token falls even as the total global demand for AI skyrockets. This falling price is what sustains the "free" model and drives the future monetization strategies.

The Subsidy Game: Keeping the Lights On

Why are AI companies still giving away technology that costs billions to build and millions to run? The answer is simple: massive subsidies.

- Cloud Partnerships: The vast majority of frontier AI models are either owned by or deeply partnered with the handful of companies that control the global cloud infrastructure (Microsoft-OpenAI, Google-Anthropic). These cloud partners don't pay the full, market rate for compute. They subsidize the AI models with billions of dollars' worth of chips and data center access. They aren't trying to make money on the AI query itself; they are trying to lock users into their cloud ecosystem. The AI model is a hook to sell cloud storage, networking, and data services.
- Venture Capital: For many independent AI startups, venture capital acts as a temporary life-support system. Investors are willing to lose money on every query today for the chance to win the market tomorrow. They are funding a land-grab. Their strategy is: scale fast, achieve dominance, and figure out the sustainable revenue model later.

For the pragmatist, this means you are operating in an economically unstable market. The free, subsidized tools you rely on today could disappear, change their terms, or raise prices dramatically the moment the companies decide their land-grab phase is over. Never rely on the free tier for a mission-critical workflow.

The Next Ad Model: From Search to Suggestion

The current internet economy is built on search. You ask a question (e.g., "best coffee maker"), and the search engine provides ten links, earning money by placing sponsored links at the top. AI is fundamentally changing this model.

When you ask an AI, "What is the best coffee maker for under

$100 that makes cold brew?" the AI doesn't give you ten links; it gives you a single, synthesized answer. This shift from search to suggestion is forcing a revolution in advertising:

- Conversational Commerce: The AI can now serve as a trusted advisor and a transaction facilitator. The inevitable next step is the rise of sponsored answers. The model might recommend the "XYZ Brand Coffee Maker" and, in the fine print, note that XYZ is a paid partner.
- Integrated Transactions: The models can easily integrate directly with e-commerce platforms, asking, "Would you like me to order that for you now?" The monetization shifts from selling ad space on a page to earning a commission on an integrated transaction.

This creates new ethical territory. How do you trust the AI's recommendation when its utility function might be split between giving you the best answer and giving its owner the most profitable answer? This requires the user to maintain an even higher degree of skepticism about the source and motivation of the information.

The Long Game: Vertical and Domain AIs

The future of sustainable AI profitability lies away from the costly, general-purpose models in the open market. The long game is the rise of the Vertical and Domain AIs—smaller, specialized, and revenue-positive models.

These are models that are fine-tuned for a specific industry (e.g., law, medicine, tax). They don't need to pass the MMLU exam; they only need to pass the Bar exam. Because they are smaller, their training and inference costs are exponentially lower. They can charge a subscription fee that is justified by the specialized, high-value insight they provide.

The monetization path is clear: offer extreme value in a narrow, high-stakes domain. These smaller models, which are often built using the open-source frameworks discussed in Chapter 21, represent the most stable and reliable path to sustainable AI profitability. They prove that efficiency and specialization, not just raw scale, are the keys to building a lasting AI business. But as efficiency and specialization define the commercial path forward, a larger question looms: what happens when intelligence itself becomes infrastructure?

The Next Phase: AI as Infrastructure

As AI becomes more deeply embedded in everything from healthcare to education to governance, it starts to resemble something else entirely—not a consumer product, but a public utility. Just as electricity, water, and the internet became essential infrastructure that governments helped fund, regulate, and distribute, AI may follow the same path.

The logic is simple: if access to advanced intelligence becomes a determinant of economic opportunity, national productivity, and even democratic participation, then universal access becomes a matter of public interest. Countries that treat AI as a strategic utility will be more resilient, innovative, and competitive.

This raises a fundamental policy question: who pays for public access to AI?

Some economists have begun to suggest that nations might need to establish AI levies or public access funds—effectively a tax-based subsidy system similar to how some countries fund healthcare. Citizens and businesses would pay into a national pool, and in return, everyone would have baseline access to secure, regulated AI systems. The government wouldn't necessarily own the AI platforms, but it might license or bulk-purchase access from private providers (OpenAI, Anthropic,

Google, etc.), much as governments today buy vaccines or cloud capacity for defense and public services.

Under this model, the "public option" for AI could coexist with private, premium versions—ensuring that no citizen is digitally excluded simply because they can't afford a subscription to the world's knowledge engine.

The implications are profound. It would mean reframing AI not as a luxury or productivity tool, but as a right of access to modern intelligence, akin to literacy or electricity. Nations that build this baseline early will create a population that's not only more productive, but also less vulnerable to manipulation and misinformation—because public AI can be audited, regulated, and kept transparent.

The Social Contract: Work, Welfare, and Universal Basic Income

If AI reshapes industries as dramatically as predicted, the other half of the economic equation isn't access—it's income.

Automation will displace certain jobs faster than it creates new ones. White-collar cognitive labor—writers, analysts, paralegals, call-center operators, even coders—will feel the squeeze first. When the marginal cost of intelligence falls toward zero, many traditional business models start to unravel. That leads to a deeper question: if humans are no longer the primary unit of productivity, how do they participate in the economy at all?

This is where Universal Basic Income (UBI) re-enters the debate—not as an ideological experiment, but as a pragmatic response to the economics of automation. If AI becomes the new labor force, it's reasonable to imagine taxing that digital labor—compute cycles, model outputs, or corporate profits derived from AI—and redistributing part of that revenue to citizens.

The idea is already being floated in various forms:

- Economists like Daron Acemoglu and Sam Altman (OpenAI's CEO) have both proposed variants of an "AI dividend", where companies that benefit most from automation contribute to a shared social fund.
- Finland, Canada, and parts of the U.S. have already trialed small-scale UBI pilots, testing how guaranteed income affects productivity, mental health, and social cohesion.
- In the long run, governments may see UBI not as welfare, but as an economic stabilizer—a way to maintain consumer demand in a post-labor economy.

UBI also raises difficult philosophical questions. If AI-generated productivity creates immense wealth, who owns that output? If algorithms replace not just human hands but human judgment, should the returns from that "synthetic workforce" belong to shareholders, or society?

The Pragmatic Middle Ground

Most likely, we will end up with a hybrid model:

- AI as a partly public utility (baseline access for all, funded via taxes or levies).
- AI as a private marketplace (premium systems, domain-specialized models, and enterprise-grade platforms competing on capability).
- And some form of redistributive mechanism, ensuring that societies remain economically stable as automation compounds.

It's a future where "Who pays for AI?" is no longer a business question, but a governance question—one that blends economics, ethics, and national strategy.

The companies building AI today might think of themselves as the next Microsofts or Googles, but they may end up as something closer to energy utilities or telecom networks – heavily regulated, indispensable, and intertwined with public policy.

The AI economy is still being propped up by subsidies and speculation. But as costs fall and capabilities expand, the real value will flow to those who treat intelligence not as a gimmick, but as infrastructure. The winners won't just be the entrepreneurs who build efficient systems – they'll be the societies that learn to distribute that power wisely.

24

AI and the Law: Copyright, IP, and Accountability

The conversation around AI is often a technical one, but arguably the most significant, and least understood, challenges are legal. As AI moves from a curious novelty to a foundational layer of business, it is colliding with a legal system built for a different time. The laws of copyright, liability, and defamation were all written with a human in mind. An author, a defendant, a speaker. The legal grey area created by AI is not a minor inconvenience; it's a strategic minefield that can lead to costly litigation, reputational damage, and, in some cases, the complete erosion of a company's intellectual property.

This chapter is about navigating that minefield. It's about understanding that the same technology that allows for incredible efficiency also introduces a new and profound set of legal risks. We'll break down the key battlegrounds where AI and the law are clashing, from the thorny question of who owns an AI-generated image to the terrifying implications of deepfakes and the complex issue of accountability when an AI system causes harm.

The Copyright Dilemma: Who Owns the Output?

AI is disrupting the realm of intellectual property (IP) by blurring the lines of authorship, ownership, and originality. Traditionally, copyright law was designed to protect works created by humans. But what happens when the work is created by a machine? This is a core challenge that has significant financial and legal implications for businesses that rely on AI-generated content.

The U.S. Copyright Office has been grappling with this issue, and its stance has been clear: AI-generated content, in and of itself, cannot receive copyright protection. The principle is that copyright protects the expression of human ideas, not works generated autonomously by machines. This means that if you use an AI tool to create a piece of art or a piece of text with minimal human input, you may not be able to claim a copyright on it. However, the line is blurry. The Copyright Office has clarified that if a human provides "significant creative input"—such as editing, arranging, or selecting AI-generated elements—the work might be eligible for protection. The extent of human involvement and the level of control are the crucial factors. For a pragmatist, this means that every AI-assisted workflow for creative output must include a clear, documented human-in-the-loop to ensure the work is legally defensible.

Training on the Internet: Fair Use or Foul Play?

The other half of the copyright dilemma is the data used to train the AI models. Most frontier models were trained on a massive corpus of data scraped from the internet, which includes millions of copyrighted works. The question is: does a model developer have the right to use this material without permission or compensation?

The legal debate hinges on the doctrine of fair use, which allows for the limited use of copyrighted material without permission for purposes like criticism, comment, news reporting, teaching, scholarship, or research. AI developers argue that using copyrighted works to extract statistical relationships and create a training library is a "transformative" use, which favors a finding of fair use. They argue that a model learning to write is like a child learning to read – it shouldn't have to pay a fee for every book it reads.

Early court decisions have provided some initial wins for AI developers on this issue, with judges finding that training models on lawfully purchased copyrighted content can be "exceedingly transformative". However, these rulings are narrow, fact-specific, and still vulnerable to appeal. A key distinction has emerged: courts are highly critical of developers who use pirated works for training, making it clear that a transformative purpose does not justify outright piracy.

For a business, this means a major risk. If you are using a third-party AI model, you are relying on the developer's legal arguments. If a court later decides that training on copyrighted material is not fair use, your AI-generated outputs could be deemed infringing, exposing you to significant legal risk. The pragmatic takeaway is to seek strong indemnification from your AI provider and to be vigilant about the provenance of the training data.

Deepfakes and Defamation: The Weaponization of AI

AI's ability to generate realistic audio, video, and images has created a new and terrifying legal battleground: deepfakes. Deepfakes can be used to impersonate or defame individuals, spread misinformation, and erode trust in media and information. While existing legal frameworks like defamation and libel laws can be used to address these harms, they are often ill-equipped for the unique challenges of AI-generated content.

The primary legal hurdles are proving intent and authenticity. Defamation laws require a plaintiff to show that a false statement was published with the intent to harm. But with deepfakes, it can be difficult to prove who created the content, especially given the anonymous nature of many creators. The line between protected speech (e.g., satire or parody) and harmful misrepresentation is also incredibly fine, particularly when it comes to public figures.

As a pragmatist, this isn't just a distant legal issue; it's a direct threat to your brand, your reputation, and your public-facing employees. The rise of deepfakes means that every piece of digital media – an interview, a product endorsement, an internal communication – can no longer be assumed to be authentic. Your legal and communications teams must be prepared to handle the reality of a fabricated crisis.

Liability in AI-Driven Decisions: Who Is to Blame?

As AI systems take on roles traditionally held by humans – from driving cars to diagnosing illnesses – the legal landscape is evolving to address the complex liability scenarios that emerge. When an AI system causes harm, who is legally at fault? Is it the developer, the deployer, the end user, or no one?

The legal system has been slow to address this, but new legal frameworks are being proposed to establish accountability. The EU has focused on a legal framework that would provide uniform rules for civil liability in cases involving AI systems, ensuring that those harmed have a clear path to protection. In the US, the approach is more fragmented, with a focus on adapting existing laws and proposing new frameworks that emphasize transparency and accountability in high-risk situations.

For a business, the pragmatic approach is to assume that accountability will ultimately rest with you. If you choose to deploy an AI system, you are responsible for its output and its consequences. This means building robust governance frameworks, conducting regular risk assessments, and ensuring that there is always a human-in-the-loop for high-stakes decisions.

A Global Patchwork: US vs. EU

The regulatory landscape is not uniform. The US and the EU are taking fundamentally different approaches, and you must be aware of both.

- The EU AI Act: The EU is focused on a comprehensive, rights-centric legal framework that uses strict, binding rules and a risk-based approach to regulate AI. It distinguishes between systems that pose an "unacceptable risk," a "high risk," and a "limited risk," with strict obligations for high-risk systems used in areas like education, healthcare, and employment. The EU AI Act (Regulation (EU) 2024/1689—Artificial Intelligence Act) is also extraterritorial, meaning it applies to any company whose AI systems are used in the EU, regardless of where they are located.
- The US Approach: The US has adopted a more fragmented, adaptive approach, relying on a patchwork of existing laws, executive orders, and agency guidance rather than a single, monolithic AI act. The focus is on fostering innovation and national security, while using existing laws to address problems as they arise. This approach can lead to legal uncertainty and a lack of clear standards.

This divergence means that global companies must navigate a complex, non-harmonized legal landscape. A policy that is compliant in one jurisdiction may be a legal risk in another.

The Future of AI Regulation: A Pragmatist's Playbook

History shows that when new technologies collide with outdated legal frameworks, courts alone are rarely enough to craft comprehensive solutions. The law will likely continue to develop through a combination of piecemeal judicial decisions, new legislative actions, and a greater emphasis on self-governance frameworks based on ethical considerations.

For the pragmatist, this creates a clear playbook for the future:

- Monitor Global Regulations: Stay informed about how different countries define AI-generated content, ownership rights, and liability.
- Establish Internal Policies: Clearly outline internal policies regarding the creation, ownership, and licensing of AI-generated content.
- Build Governance Frameworks: Create robust AI governance frameworks that can be adapted to jurisdictional requirements. This includes conducting regular risk assessments, ensuring human oversight, and fostering transparency with stakeholders.

The law isn't a passive set of rules; it's a living, breathing system. Your job as a leader is to be an active participant in its evolution by building the internal policies and ethical frameworks that protect your business and shape a more responsible future.

25

The End of the Garage Myth

If the story of technology had a creation myth, it would begin in a garage. Bill Gates and Paul Allen hunched over code for a scrappy new operating system. Steve Jobs and Steve Wozniak soldering the first Apple computer on a wooden table. Mark Zuckerberg building Facebook from a Harvard dorm room. These were the original archetypes of the modern entrepreneur—the small team with a big idea, turning curiosity into empires with little more than pizza, caffeine, and a conviction that the future could be different.

For decades, this was the template. Great revolutions began in small rooms. The internet was the great equalizer: a platform that flattened hierarchy, lowered barriers, and let anyone with talent and tenacity build something that could change the world.

But AI—at least the version of it that dominates headlines and stock markets—has rewritten that script.

The Basement Is Closed (for Now)

Let's start with a hard truth: you can't build GPT-4 in your garage. The age of the basement breakthrough has, for the moment, been priced out of existence. Training a frontier model today—one that competes at the level of GPT-4, Claude 3 Opus, or Gemini 1.5 Pro—costs hundreds of millions of dollars in compute alone. Add the cost of data licensing, energy, engineers, and infrastructure, and the bill can easily climb above $500 million for a single training run.

The hardware requirements are staggering.

Training a large model typically means tens of thousands of top-end GPUs, networked together in clusters so dense they consume megawatts of power. These chips are scarce, expensive, and often subject to export controls. They live in data centers built like fortresses, cooled by industrial chillers, guarded by biometric scanners. Not exactly the kind of setup you can rig up beside the lawnmower.

So the romantic vision of two friends in a garage, bootstrapping the next computing revolution, doesn't fit this world. Not because creativity is dead, but because the playing field has tilted toward capital.

The garage myth was powered by a different kind of physics.

Back then, the costs of innovation were falling. Microprocessors were cheap. The internet was open. Anyone could learn to code, publish a website, or reach millions of people from a bedroom. The raw material of innovation—information—was free or nearly so.

AI is different. Its raw material is compute, not code. And compute has gravity.

The New Platform Hierarchy

Every great wave of technology has its own hierarchy.

In the 1980s and 1990s, it was operating systems—Windows and Mac.

In the 2000s, it was search engines and social networks—Google and Facebook.

Today, in the 2020s, it's models—GPT, Gemini, Claude, Mistral.

That means the new platform layers look like this:

- AI is the new Internet. It's the global infrastructure, the invisible substrate that will underpin everything from education to entertainment to healthcare.
- Large Language Models (LLMs) are the new Operating Systems. They are the interface between human intention and machine capability, the layer through which everything else will run.
- The next great companies will be the Apps. They'll build on top of these models, not beneath them.

And that's where the hope comes back in.

Because while you can't train the next GPT in your garage, you can build the next billion-dollar company using it. The magic of AI is not just in its scale—it's in its leverage.

A solo developer with a smart idea can now automate design, marketing, customer support, and even the coding itself. A startup of five can do the work of fifty. The constraint has shifted from money to imagination.

What the New "Garage" Looks Like

The modern garage isn't a place—it's a layer. It's a Discord server full of open-source hackers building agents that chain together multiple models to perform complex tasks.

It's a Substack community where prompt engineers are refining "recipes" that let small teams outperform corporate systems.

It's a low-cost API call to OpenAI or Anthropic that gives a 17-year-old in Manila or Lagos access to the same intelligence layer as Google.

The "garage" has gone global and virtual.

Today's scrappy innovators are building copilots, autonomous agents, and workflow assistants that sit on top of the big models. They're finding the hidden seams—those narrow, unexplored spaces between what the models can do and what people actually need done.

This is where the next wave of giants will emerge.

Not by owning the model, but by owning the relationship between the model and the human.

When the Apps Become the Ecosystem

Think back to the early internet. At first, the platform itself was the story: "You can go online!" Then came the websites, the browsers, the marketplaces, and eventually, the social networks that captured the world's attention. The infrastructure faded into the background, and the experience became the product.

AI is following that same arc.

Right now, the models—GPT, Claude, Gemini—get all the attention. But soon, the focus will shift to how they are used: the interfaces, the services, the ecosystems that turn general intelligence into personal utility.

Just as Windows created space for Word and Excel, and the iPhone created space for Instagram and Uber, the major models are creating a foundation for a flood of new applications.

These "apps" may not look like apps at all. They might be conversational agents that live across your devices. They might be AI colleagues that manage parts of your business. They might be invisible systems embedded in cars, factories, schools, and hospitals.

And just as before, the biggest winners won't necessarily be the ones who build the platform—they'll be the ones who build on it.

Why the Next OpenAI Won't Look Like OpenAI

The next great AI company might not build a model at all. Instead, it might master orchestration—the ability to combine multiple models, APIs, and data sources into seamless experiences. Think of it as the "director" role in an AI orchestra, deciding which model plays when, and for what purpose.

Or it might dominate through data gravity: controlling the flow of real-world information that keeps other systems learning.

Or distribution: owning the channels where AI actually meets users—voice, chat, productivity tools, gaming, entertainment.

In other words, the new empires will be built not through raw horsepower but through integration, trust, and context.

This opens a door back to creativity. Because those are things individuals and small teams can still do better than corporations.

The Return of the Tinkerers

Even within the constraints of scale, the spirit of the garage never really dies—it just evolves.

Open-source models like LLaMA, Mistral, Falcon, and Mixtral have reintroduced the spirit of democratization. They may not be quite as powerful as GPT-4 or Claude 3, but they're good enough to build meaningful applications—and you can fine-tune them on your laptop.

A small team can take an open model, specialize it for a niche—legal summaries, climate science, therapy chat, coding workflows—and create something genuinely useful without touching the frontier.

This is how disruption sneaks back in through the side door. The frontier is sealed off, but the frontier's outputs are open for remixing. The next wave of garage inventors won't train models; they'll compose them.

And that act of composition—building, chaining, fine-tuning—is becoming the new form of creativity.

We used to solder circuits; now we connect APIs. We used to write assembly code; now we write prompts. We used to build hardware; now we build interfaces for thought.

The Real Bottleneck: Human Vision

In the age of AI, capital is abundant, compute is constrained, and creativity is the scarcest resource.

Everyone can access the same intelligence layer, but not everyone can imagine something new to do with it. That's where the next "garage" stories will come from—not the technically brilliant, but the humanly insightful.

The real breakthroughs will happen at the intersection of need and empathy.

An educator building an AI that speaks in the dialects her students actually understand.

A healthcare worker designing a tool to translate patient data into plain language.

A small business owner training a micro-agent to run her marketing overnight.

Each of these is small, local, human—but in aggregate, they'll define the next decade of AI far more than the release of GPT-6.

When the Cycle Turns Again

History tells us that monopolies never last.

The same forces that once made the garage powerful—falling costs, open platforms, and shared knowledge—will eventually circle back.

Model compression, quantization, and distillation are already shrinking models by orders of magnitude without losing performance. Synthetic data generation is reducing the need for vast human-labeled datasets.

At some point, the tools that today require a supercomputer

will fit in a backpack.

And when that happens, the garages will open again.

But this time, they won't just be in Silicon Valley. They'll be in Nairobi, São Paulo, Kuala Lumpur, and Warsaw. Innovation will decentralize just as intelligence itself has.

The myth will return—but it won't look like it used to.

It will be distributed, multilingual, and collective.

Closing Reflection

The end of the garage myth isn't the end of creativity. It's the end of nostalgia for a kind of innovation that depended on scarcity—scarcity of access, of knowledge, of opportunity.

AI's story begins at scale, but it will end in distribution. The same forces that make frontier models unreachable also make their capabilities universally available.

So maybe the question isn't who can afford to build the next great model. Maybe it's who can imagine the next great use for it. Because in the end, revolutions don't start with machines. They start with someone who looks at the machine and thinks, "What else could this do?"

PART 5
LOOKING FORWARD

We've come a long way. We started by dissecting a single, misleading word, and we've ended by looking at the global geopolitical landscape of technology. We've journeyed from the psychology of the First Try Trap to the practicalities of a well-crafted prompt.

The goal of this book was never to convince you that AI is perfect. It was to convince you that perfection is the wrong goal. The goal is progress. It's about being a little more creative, a little more efficient, and a little more insightful than you were yesterday.

This final section is about what comes next. How do we take the lessons from this book and apply them tomorrow morning? We'll look at the future of human-AI collaboration, the enduring role of skepticism, and, most importantly, provide a simple, practical playbook for you to start your own journey with confidence.

Before we begin the final leg of our journey, let's return to the central metaphor: If technology is a movie, not a snapshot, why do so many insist on judging a single frame instead of the whole reel?

BEYOND HALLUCINATIONS

26

Beyond Errors, Toward Collaboration

For most of this book, we've talked about AI as a tool. A power drill, a calculator for words, a tireless intern. It's a useful metaphor, but it's also becoming an outdated one. The next phase of this technology is not about using a better tool. It's about gaining a new kind of partner.

What's the difference? You direct a tool. You collaborate with a partner. A tool executes a command. A partner understands your intent. The evolution from tool to partner is the single most important shift in how we will work with AI in the coming years, and it will fundamentally reshape what we believe is possible.

As we talk about AI evolving from a simple cog into a true partner, it's impossible to ignore the elephant in the room: Artificial General Intelligence (AGI).

This is the big, sci-fi idea of an AI that can think, learn, and reason across a vast range of domains, essentially matching or exceeding human intelligence in every way. The step beyond that is Artificial Super Intelligence (ASI)—an intellect so far beyond our own it's hard to even imagine. It's a fascinating, and frankly, dizzying topic for researchers and futurists.

But for us? For the leaders, creators, and professionals trying to solve today's problems and hit tomorrow's targets? Obsessing over a hypothetical super-intelligence is a strategic mistake. It's like planning for a colony on Mars when you haven't figured out how to build a reliable car.

The window of opportunity that's closing isn't about AGI. It's about mastering the powerful, practical AI we have right now. The work that will define the winners and losers of the next decade isn't about waiting for a sentient machine. It's about the pragmatic, and often unglamorous, job of building reliable systems where AI can act as a trusted partner.

From Tool to Partner: The Age of Agents

Think about the difference between a hammer and a master carpenter's apprentice. You use a hammer to hit a nail. You tell it what to do, and it does it. An apprentice, on the other hand, learns your style. They anticipate your needs. You can give them a high-level goal, like "help me build this frame," and they can figure out the intermediate steps. They might even suggest a better way to do it.

Today's AI is like a very good hammer. Tomorrow's AI is that apprentice. We are moving from a world of single-shot prompts—call-and-response—to a world of what the industry calls "agents". An AI agent is a system that can take a complex, multi-step goal, break it down into a series of tasks, use various tools to execute those tasks, and then report back on its progress.

The shift is monumental. You are no longer just a prompter; you are a manager, delegating complex projects to a team of tireless, instantaneous digital colleagues.

- Today: "Write me an email to my sales team about our Q3 results."
- Tomorrow: "Analyze our latest sales data from the CRM, identify the top three performing regions and the bottom three, summarize the key takeaways from the earnings call transcript, and draft a presentation for next week's all-

hands meeting that celebrates the wins and outline a plan for the underperforming regions."

These agent-based workflows are not science fiction; they are being built right now. They represent a monumental shift in leverage.

What's Next for Human-AI Workflows

This shift from tool to partner changes everything about our workflows. The nature of our collaboration deepens in three key ways:

- From Prompting to Briefing: Our interactions will look less like a series of commands and more like a creative brief. We'll spend our time defining the goal, the constraints, the audience, and the desired tone, and then let the AI agent figure out the execution. Our value will be in our strategic direction, not our tactical input.
- AI-to-AI Collaboration: The most powerful workflows will involve multiple specialized AI agents working together. Imagine an "analyst" agent that pulls data, a "writer" agent that drafts a report, and a "critic" agent that pokes holes in the argument—all before a human ever sees the first draft. This is about creating an intelligent assembly line, where each agent contributes its specific skill to a common goal.
- Proactive Assistance: Your AI partner won't just wait for your command. It will learn your patterns and proactively offer help. It might notice you have a big presentation coming up and automatically gather the relevant research. It might see you're struggling to write an email and offer a better phrasing. This is a world where the friction between idea and execution is reduced almost to zero.

New Collaboration Models for Business

For entrepreneurs and business leaders, this new era of collaboration creates a massive landscape of opportunity. The barrier to entry for building a business has been dramatically lowered. You no longer need to hire a full team to start. You can build a "digital team" of AI agents to do the work.

Here are some examples of what this looks like in practice:

- The Content Engine: Instead of hiring a writer, an SEO expert, and a social media manager, you can collaborate with a suite of AI agents. A content creation agent can generate SEO-optimized articles and social media posts. Another agent can analyze trends to suggest new topics. A third can schedule posts for optimal engagement times and create caption variations for different platforms. The human's job becomes one of a creative director: setting the strategy, refining the voice, and adding the personal touch that only you can provide.
- The Sales Prospecting Team: A business development agent can automate the tedious process of lead generation by identifying potential customers on social media. A prospecting agent can then generate and send personalized outreach emails at scale, and even book qualified meetings directly to your calendar. This frees up your human sales team to focus on what they do best: building relationships and closing deals.
- The Full-Stack Marketing Agency: You can create an entire agency with a few humans and a powerful suite of AI agents. An AI-powered platform can automate workflows, from email marketing to social media management. You can use agents to conduct market research, perform competitive analysis, and automate A/B testing for campaigns, which

previously would have taken months to perfect. The humans on your team become strategists, analysts, and creative directors, while the agents handle the execution.

This is a world where a small business can have the capabilities of a large enterprise, and where a single person can launch a business that once required a team of ten. The goal isn't just to work faster; it's to work smarter and with greater leverage.

AI as Creative Catalyst

This brings us to the most exciting frontier of all: creativity. If an AI partner can handle the grunt work of research, analysis, and first drafts, what does that free us up to do?

It frees us to be more human. It gives us more time for the deep thinking, the unexpected connections, and the flashes of insight that machines can't replicate. An AI can generate a thousand marketing slogans, but it can't have the conversation with a customer that reveals a deep, unmet need. An AI can analyze a million data points, but it can't have the gut feeling that a new market is about to open up.

The true promise of this collaborative future isn't that the AI will do our thinking for us. It's that it will free us from the mundane, repetitive, and time-consuming tasks that so often get in the way of our best thinking. It is, perhaps for the first time, a tool that can help us overcome not just the blank page, but the cluttered mind. The goal is not to reduce our reliance on human error, but to increase our capacity for human brilliance.

27

AND THE WINNER IS...

Every few months, a headline declares that someone has won the AI race.

OpenAI releases a new model. Google unveils a competitor. Elon Musk announces a project with a single cryptic tweet. The news cycle erupts with superlatives: faster, smarter, cheaper, better. CEOs talk about "pulling ahead." Governments talk about "falling behind." Investors talk about "staking their claim."

The tone is unmistakably competitive—as if Artificial Intelligence were an Olympic event, a global relay where one company or country will break the tape while the rest applaud from the stands. But that framing, seductive as it sounds, is deeply flawed.

Because what if AI isn't a race at all? What if it's an ecosystem—less a sprint to the finish line, and more a rainforest of interconnected systems growing, competing, and cross-pollinating in unpredictable ways?

If that's true, then the question "Who wins?" misses the point entirely. The better question might be: how does winning even work in a world where intelligence is no longer scarce?

The Myth of the Finish Line

Winner-takes-all markets are familiar stories in technology.

The internet had its Google. Social media had its Facebook. Smartphones had their Apple. Each cycle crowned one or two companies that built the best flywheel—the network effect that turned size into an almost unbreakable moat.

For years, many assumed AI would follow the same pattern. After all, the logic fits: the more data you have, the better your models get; the better your models, the more users you attract; the more users you attract, the more data you have. The feedback loop seems inevitable—a self-reinforcing cycle of dominance.

That logic underpins the winner-takes-all hypothesis. It's tidy, powerful, and wrong in all the most interesting ways.

AI isn't a single market, and intelligence isn't a single product. The "AI race" isn't about who gets to AGI first—it's about who finds the most value along the way. The truth is closer to winner-takes-most-within-context—where different players dominate specific layers, domains, or geographies of the AI stack.

Why Winner-Takes-All Doesn't Fit Anymore

The biggest reason the AI race won't crown a single champion is that its raw material—data and compute—doesn't behave like oil or land or users. It doesn't sit still.

In classic monopolies, power compounds because every new user strengthens the moat. Facebook's network effect grew with each friend request. Google's ad engine improved with every click. But AI data is fragmented. Health data in Germany can't legally train a model in the U.S. Text data in China is censored differently than in France. Corporate data stays locked behind firewalls. There is no single "ocean" of data to dominate—only a patchwork of local lakes.

And even where data flows freely, the returns to scale are flattening. Between 2012 and 2018, compute for frontier models doubled every 3.4 months—ten times faster than Moore's Law.

But after 2022, that curve began to slow. Models kept getting bigger, but not dramatically better. The exponential gains that once justified trillion-dollar bets are beginning to yield to diminishing returns.

That means size alone is no longer destiny. The next breakthroughs won't come from sheer volume—they'll come from focus. From domain knowledge. From applying intelligence to places where it matters most.

Which leads to a new reality: AI doesn't have one winner—it has many.

Four Possible Winners

Depending on how the next decade unfolds, we may see four very different kinds of winners emerge—each one powerful, each one operating on a different layer of the AI value chain.

1. The Infrastructure Winners

These are the quiet giants: Nvidia, TSMC, and the cloud providers like AWS, Google Cloud, and Microsoft Azure. They don't build the brains; they build the bodies. Without them, nothing runs. Chips, servers, power—the hardware that fuels the algorithms.

In many ways, they've already won. Every time a new model launches, it feeds demand for more GPUs, more data centers, more cooling systems. The profit margins flow upstream. In the short term, the infrastructure players are the most tangible winners of the AI boom.

But they also carry the most risk. They're tied to massive capital expenditure and vulnerable to political interference—export controls, resource bottlenecks, and energy scarcity. Their dominance is real, but it's physical, not intellectual.

2. The Model Winners

These are the headline-makers—OpenAI, Anthropic, Google DeepMind, xAI, Mistral, Cohere. They compete to build the biggest, smartest, most general-purpose model on Earth.

Their prize is prestige—and platform control. A frontier model acts as a gravitational center: everything orbits it. Apps, plugins, and products rely on their APIs, and that interdependence creates leverage. But these companies face a paradox: their best customers are also their biggest competitors. Every developer fine-tuning a model is, in a small way, eroding their moat.

The next generation of models may be smaller, specialized, and locally run—the opposite of what "frontier" implies. When anyone can download a 15B parameter model that runs on a laptop and performs well enough for 80% of use cases, the advantage of owning a trillion-parameter model starts to fade.

3. The Platform Winners

These are the companies that control the interfaces—the front doors to everyday life. Microsoft, Apple, Google, Meta, and Amazon are already embedding AI into their ecosystems so deeply that users barely notice it's there.

In this world, winning isn't about having the smartest model; it's about being the default. When you dictate the operating system, the browser, or the workplace productivity suite, your model doesn't have to be perfect—just omnipresent.

If history repeats, the platform layer could become the most durable monopoly of all. People switch apps easily, but they rarely switch ecosystems. A model might answer your question, but a platform owns your workflow.

4. The Domain Winners

Finally, the quiet specialists—the companies applying AI to specific industries where depth beats scale. Think of medical imaging startups, legal analysis platforms, design assistants, or wellness concierges.

These models don't need the whole internet; they need precision, context, and credibility. A radiology AI trained on millions of verified scans doesn't care about Shakespeare or Stack Overflow. Its strength is its boundaries.

The beauty of this layer is resilience. Domain winners can thrive beneath the giants, borrowing infrastructure, leasing models, and building trust in niches the big players can't afford to specialize in. In the long run, they may prove to be the most sustainable businesses in the entire stack.

A Mosaic of Monopolies

So who wins? All of them—and none of them.

The future of AI won't resemble the monolithic dominance of Google Search or Windows. It will look more like a mosaic of overlapping monopolies, each owning its patch of territory: compute, model, platform, domain.

And that fragmentation isn't a flaw; it's a form of resilience. When intelligence becomes decentralized, innovation becomes anti-fragile. Power distributes itself naturally, pulled toward the edges where human context matters most.

It's tempting to see AI as a single race, but it's better understood as a cascade of interlocking competitions—some global, some national, some hyperlocal. China might dominate state-scale AI; the U.S. might lead in research; Europe might lead in regulation; Africa and Southeast Asia might innovate in applied AI, skipping legacy stages the way they leapfrogged landlines for mobile.

This isn't a single finish line. It's a constantly shifting network of advantage.

Why Geography Still Matters

Despite the global reach of cloud computing, AI remains constrained by borders.

Data sovereignty laws, censorship regimes, and privacy frameworks all act as invisible fences. The EU's AI Act shapes what can be built in Europe. U.S. export controls shape what chips can reach China. Nations are beginning to build not just their own armies and currencies, but their own models of intelligence.

We're entering an era of digital mercantilism, where countries hoard data the way they once hoarded oil. The race isn't just to build smarter machines, but to ensure that intelligence reflects local values and political goals.

That makes "winner-takes-all" not only unrealistic, but impossible. The future is "winner-per-country, winner-per-context."

The AI ecosystem will look less like a pyramid and more like a map—clusters of influence connected by APIs instead of trade routes.

The Human Layer: The Real Prize

There's one more kind of winner that rarely makes the headlines: us.

The individuals, teams, and organizations who learn to integrate AI effectively—not as a gimmick, but as a genuine cognitive partner—will win in ways that outlast any model release cycle.

The true differentiator won't be access to the latest model; it will be literacy—knowing how to frame questions, interpret answers, and design workflows that blend human judgment with machine speed.

In that sense, "winning" the AI race is less about building

intelligence and more about absorbing it. The nations, companies, and people who do that best—who turn intelligence into competence—will quietly outpace everyone else.

The Pragmatist's View

For all the noise about competition, AI may turn out to be one of the least zero-sum technologies ever invented. Every advance eventually becomes public knowledge. Every paper, every model, every open-weight release raises the tide. Even the closed systems can't stay sealed for long—their innovations diffuse, copied, adapted, democratized.

So maybe the real winners aren't the ones racing to own intelligence, but the ones building with it. The entrepreneurs, educators, and experimenters who turn the abstract promise of AI into everyday impact.

In the end, AI isn't a horse race—it's a relay. Each generation builds on the last, passing the baton forward. No one runs the whole distance alone.

And when the dust settles, there won't be one podium or one medal ceremony. There will just be billions of people, each holding a slightly different version of the same tool—each finding their own way to win.

Closing Reflection

The idea that one company, one country, or one model will "win AI" is comforting because it gives chaos a champion. It makes the future feel predictable, maybe even safe. But intelligence doesn't work that way. It expands, fragments, and adapts faster than anyone can contain it.

The real victory won't belong to whoever crosses the line first, but to those who learn how to build something meaningful with what we've already created—tools that endure, systems that serve, progress that compounds quietly rather than conquers loudly.

28

The Future of Skepticism

So, the future is a glorious partnership. We'll all have brilliant AI apprentices, our productivity will skyrocket, and our creativity will be unleashed. Right? Not so fast. Every technological revolution in history has been met with a wall of skepticism, and this one is no different. For every person who embraces this new world of collaboration, there will be another who dismisses it, fears it, or actively resists it. And frankly, they'll have some very good reasons. As pragmatists, we can't just ignore the skeptics. We have to understand where they're coming from. Because if we don't, our brilliant, collaborative future will remain the property of a few early adopters, while the rest of the world gets left behind.

The Four Faces of Dismissal

Skepticism isn't a single, monolithic thing. It comes in many flavors, each demanding a different response. You can't address all these groups with the same argument.

- The Burned Believer: This is the person who is stuck in the First Try Trap we talked about in Chapter 4. They tried an early version—maybe it hallucinated a fake legal case or generated unusable code—it failed them, and they've built an identity around knowing "the truth" about AI.

Their skepticism is a shield protecting them from the acute embarrassment of a failure. The risk here is organizational inertia: a leader or key manager makes a permanent policy based on one early, bad data point, effectively banning the future of a crucial technology. You can't argue with their data; you have to show them new data.

- The Threatened Expert: This is the person whose professional identity is deeply tied to the very tasks that AI is beginning to automate. The master copywriter who sees their craft being devalued. The seasoned financial analyst whose complex data-crunching skills are suddenly obsolete. Their skepticism is a form of self-preservation. Telling them they'll be "more productive" only deepens their fear that they are being replaced. You are not just threatening their workflow; you are threatening their sense of professional worth. This is the hardest type of skepticism to overcome, as it requires a fundamental identity shift.
- The Principled Objector: This is the person with legitimate ethical concerns about bias, job displacement, or the concentration of power in the hands of a few tech companies. Their skepticism is a moral stance. They are not afraid of the work; they are afraid of the consequences of the work. Telling them the AI is "faster" will miss their point entirely. They are raising the ethical fire alarms, often performing a vital, unpaid risk assessment for your organization. Ignore them at your peril.
- The Simply Overwhelmed: This is perhaps the largest group of all. They are busy, stressed, and being told they have to learn yet another new technology. Their skepticism is a form of exhaustion. They don't have the mental space to engage in a revolution. They will default to their old, comfortable, predictable workflows, even if they are demonstrably

slower. Their resistance isn't malice; it's bandwidth protection. They need the path of least resistance to be the path of AI adoption.

The Cost of Inertia: Why Skepticism Must Be Engaged

When skeptics are ignored, they don't just stay put; they become drag anchors on the organization. This inertia carries real, quantifiable costs:

- Loss of Competitive Edge: While your team is arguing about whether AI works, your competitor is launching an AI-generated product line, optimizing their supply chain, or tripling their marketing output. The AI gap widens daily.
- Talent Drain: Your most curious, future-focused employees will leave if they see the organization actively resisting the cutting edge. They won't tolerate being forced to use yesterday's tools to solve tomorrow's problems.
- Unmitigated Risk: The principled skeptic who flags a potential bias in your hiring algorithm could save you a massive lawsuit. By silencing the skeptical voice, you remove your most valuable internal defense mechanism against ethical and legal failure. Skepticism is free quality assurance.

How to Engage Skeptics Constructively

So what do you do? You don't win a debate with a skeptic by throwing facts at them. You win them over by solving a problem for them. The lesson from the Rescue Stories in Chapter 18 is the most important one in this book. Adoption doesn't happen through grand, top-down mandates. It happens one small, practical, undeniable success at a time.

1. Don't Talk About the Technology; Talk About the Friction.

Find the most annoying, time-consuming, low-value part of their day and show them a workflow that can help. This is the low-stakes, high-leverage move.

- For the Overwhelmed: Instead of demanding they learn "prompt engineering," show them how a saved, two-click AI workflow can summarize a 50-email chain they were dreading. Is it summarizing meetings? Is it chasing late payments? Is it analyzing customer feedback? Start with the pain.
- The Strategy: Frame the AI as a relief valve, not a taskmaster. Emphasize that the tool will absorb the busywork, the mechanical repetition that they hate, freeing them for the work that is truly valuable and human.

2. Start with Augmentation, Not Replacement (The Identity Shift).

The Threatened Expert needs a new job title, even if it's informal. Frame the AI as an assistant that helps them do their existing job better, not as a replacement for their expertise.

- Reframing Expertise: Tell the copywriter, "The AI writes the drafts, but you are the voice of the brand, the final judge of tone, and the strategic curator of emotional resonance." Tell the analyst, "The AI crunches the million data points, but you are the one who tells the story, interprets the anomaly, and makes the strategic recommendation."
- The New Role: Your job is to promote them from Doer to Editor-in-Chief. The AI handles the mechanics; the human owns the judgment, the context, and the consequence. This is an elevation, not a demotion.

3. Make It Safe to Experiment (The Sandbox Approach).
Create low-stakes sandboxes where people can try these tools without fear of failure or judgment. This is vital for the Burned Believer.

- De-Risking Failure: Set up a dedicated, non-client-facing space where any hallucination is funny, not catastrophic. Encourage them to try to break the AI. The failure is the learning. .
- Visible Scoreboards: Track successful uses (e.g., "Time Saved on Drafts," "Number of Ideas Generated"). Make the positive impact visible, not just the potential for error. This allows them to overcome the negative stickiness of their first failure with a stack of small, recent wins.

4. The Strategic Value of Doubt: Your Internal Red Team
Here's the radical idea: stop seeing the skeptic as a problem to be fixed and start seeing them as a feature to be activated. The most naturally skeptical people in your organization are your best defense against an over-confident AI. They are your internal Red Team.

- **Red Teaming with Skeptics:** When you roll out a new AI application—say, a legal brief generator or a predictive market tool—don't give it to the early adopters. Give it to your most vocal critics. Task them not with using the tool, but with breaking it. Ask them: "Find the flaws. Make it hallucinate. Force it to expose its bias." This formalizes their skepticism into a value-add role.
- **Improving the Golden Set:** The questions a skeptic asks are often far more incisive than those an optimist asks. Use their toughest, most cynical prompts to continuously test and improve your AI's Golden Set (Chapter 8). The questions they ask expose the edge cases and blind spots

that an enthusiast would never look for.

- **Mandatory Dissent:** Build a process where a skeptical sign-off is required before deploying high-stakes AI. This gives the Principled Objector a formal voice and ensures that ethical and risk considerations are baked into the process, not bolted on at the end.

The goal isn't to force everyone to become an AI expert. The goal is to make the technology so quietly useful in the background that they barely notice it's there. Like the spell-checker in your word processor, it just becomes part of the way work gets done.

Ultimately, the best antidote to both blind hype and cynical skepticism is a simple mindset: pragmatic curiosity. It's the willingness to ask, "What if this could help?" It's the discipline to test that question with small, controlled experiments. It's the wisdom to accept the results, good or bad, and adjust your approach accordingly. A pragmatically curious person doesn't believe the hype, but they don't dismiss the potential either. They treat every new development not as a threat or a salvation, but as an opportunity to learn. They are not optimists or pessimists. They are scientists in their own domain. This is the mindset that will separate the winners from the losers in the coming decade. The future doesn't belong to the loudest evangelist or the harshest critic. It belongs to the quiet experimenter.

29

A Playbook for the Curious

This book was designed to change your mind. This chapter is designed to change your behaviour. We've covered a lot of ground, from the technical to the psychological to the geopolitical. But theory without action is just a story we tell ourselves. The only way to truly move beyond the hallucinations is to roll up your sleeves and start building the workflows that work for you.

This is your playbook. It's a set of simple, practical, and safe ways to start your journey. No jargon. No hype. Just a clear, step-by-step guide to becoming a pragmatically curious experimenter, starting today.

The "Beyond the Hallucinations" Mindset: A 5-Point Checklist

Before you start any experiment, remind yourself of the core principles. This is your mental toolkit.

1. **Calibrate Your Trust.** Is this a high-stakes or a low-stakes task? Adjust your skepticism accordingly. Never grant blind trust. The stakes dictate the necessary level of oversight. If you're writing a first draft for an internal memo, the trust dial can be turned way up. If you're drafting a legal brief, the dial should be at zero until you've manually verified every single statement. The tool is only as reliable as the system you build around it.

2. **Use the Right Tool for the Job.** Is this a fact-finding mission or a creative brainstorm? A general chatbot is not a reliable search engine. Use systems with grounding and citations (RAG) for facts. Don't use a screwdriver to hammer a nail. For a quick headline brainstorm, a large-scale, general model is perfect. For summarizing a confidential financial report, a fine-tuned, private model running on your own data is a sensible choice. The technology's capability is only half the story; your strategic application of it is the other half.
3. **Brief Like a Manager, Not a Magician.** Don't use cryptic one-liners. Provide role, task, context, and format. The quality of your output is a direct reflection of the quality of your input. Instead of saying, "Write me an email," try: "Act as my marketing assistant. Your task is to draft a polite but firm email to a client who is late on their payment. The context is that this is their third late payment. The format should be a draft email that I can quickly edit and send." This level of detail isn't about being picky; it's about being professional.
4. **You are the Editor-in-Chief**. The AI generates the first draft. You are responsible for the final product. Your expertise is the most important part of the process. Your job shifts from filling a blank page to curating and editing a first draft. This is a much higher-value use of your time. Embrace the 80/20 rule: the AI gives you the first 80% quickly, and you add the crucial 20% of judgment, nuance, and verification that only a human can provide.
5. **Look for Leverage, Not Magic.** Don't try to solve your biggest, hairiest problem on day one. Find a small, repetitive, high-friction task and see if AI can give you back 10 minutes in your day. That's a win. The path to real value is paved with small, repeatable successes, not with one

giant, risky leap. Think of it as a "10-minute audit." Where do you lose 10 minutes every day? Can AI give that time back to you? Start there.

Experiments You Can Try in 30 minutes

Ready to start? Here are three simple, low-risk experiments you can run right now. Pick one. Set a timer for thirty minutes. Don't aim for perfection. Aim for a result that is "better than nothing."

Experiment #1: The Meeting Master

- The Goal: Reclaim the time you lose to meeting admin.
- The Task: Take a transcript or a detailed set of notes from your last meeting. Paste it into an AI tool.
- The Prompt: "Act as my executive assistant. Please summarize the key decisions made in this meeting and create a bulleted list of all action items, with the owner of each item clearly identified."
- The Test: How does the AI's summary compare to your own? Did it capture the action items correctly? Could this save you time next week? Now, imagine scaling this up. What if every meeting in your company had a perfect, auto-generated summary? What problems would that solve?

Experiment #2: The Devil's Advocate

- The Goal: Pressure-test one of your own ideas.
- The Task: Take an idea you're currently working on—a proposal, a new project plan, a draft of an important email. Briefly summarize it.
- The Prompt: "Act as a highly critical and skeptical business consultant. My idea is [your summary here]. What are the three biggest flaws or weaknesses in this idea that I might be missing?"
- The Test: Did the AI identify a genuine blind spot? Did its

critique force you to strengthen your argument? Consider this: an AI will never get tired of playing devil's advocate. It will never worry about hurting your feelings. It will give you the unvarnished critique you need to build a better argument.

Experiment #3: The Five-Minute Analyst

- The Goal: Find the signal in the noise of your own data.
- The Task: Gather a small, anonymous sample of qualitative data you have access to. This could be a dozen customer reviews, a handful of support tickets, or comments from a recent employee survey.
- The Prompt: "Act as a data analyst. I am providing you with [type of data]. Please read through all of it and identify the top 3 most common positive themes and the top 3 most common negative themes."
- The Test: Did the AI spot a pattern you hadn't noticed before? Could this workflow, scaled up, provide valuable insights for your team? This is about using the AI to do the boring work of reading through a mountain of text, so you can do the high-value work of making a strategic decision.

A Final Invitation

This playbook isn't the end of the book. It's the beginning of your next chapter.

The pace of change in artificial intelligence is staggering, and it can be tempting to simply wait on the sidelines until things "settle down." But they won't. This is the new normal. The movie is already playing.

You don't need to be an expert. You don't need to have all the answers. You just need to be willing to ask the questions. You just need to be curious. And if you don't know how to do that, just ask the AI.

So, go ahead. Pick an experiment. Open a new tab.

And look again.

Epilogue: The Photograph and the Movie

We began this journey by calling out the "First Try Trap," the psychological shortcut that convinces so many smart, capable people to judge a fast-moving revolution by a single, grainy photograph from its opening credits. I told you that judging today's artificial intelligence based on a disappointing experience a year or two ago is like dismissing modern filmmaking because you once saw a silent, black-and-white movie and found it lacking.

AI is like a movie. It's a technology that is evolving so quickly that what was true six months ago might be irrelevant today. It's a continuous reel of new capabilities, new risks, and new opportunities, and you can't understand it by looking at a single frame.

So, now that we're at the end of the book, what's your next move?

Will you walk away with the knowledge you've gained and file it away for later? Will you let the knowledge calcify, allowing this moment in time to become another static photograph in your mind?

Or will you do the hard, necessary work of watching the rest of the movie?

The real challenge of working with AI isn't about understanding the technology. It's about updating your own mental models as the technology evolves. It's about being willing to set aside the comfort of your first impression and look again. It's about building a practice of pragmatic curiosity—a mindset that doesn't blindly believe the hype but also doesn't dismiss the potential. It's a mindset that is willing to ask, "What if this could help?" and then test that question with small, controlled experiments.

The most dangerous thing you can do right now isn't to make a mistake with AI. It's to stop searching for answers. It's to assume you have a complete picture when you've only seen a single frame.

The movie is still playing. So, stay in the theatre. Keep watching. And keep building. Stay pragmatically curious.

A Final Thought: If Asimov Were Here Today

When the science-fiction writer Isaac Asimov first introduced his Three Laws of Robotics in the 1942 short story "Runaround" (part of I, Robot), the word robot still meant something made of metal and gears.

His goal wasn't to predict the future of technology – it was to ask a moral question: If we build something that can act, how do we make sure it acts for good?

Asimov's Original Three Laws of Robotics (1942)

1. A robot may not injure a human being, or, through inaction, allow a human being to come to harm.
2. A robot must obey the orders given it by human beings, except where such orders would conflict with the First Law.
3. A robot must protect its own existence as long as such protection does not conflict with the First or Second Law.

Decades later, Asimov added a "Zeroth Law" – a rule placed above all others:

A robot may not harm humanity, or, by inaction, allow humanity to come to harm.

Those fictional laws were written for a world of visible machines—not invisible intelligence running silently in the cloud. Yet the same question still stands: how do we ensure that what we create amplifies human values rather than erodes them?

If Asimov were alive today, watching large language models learn to write, speak, and decide, he might revise his laws for a world where the robot no longer has a body, but a voice.

Asimov's Laws of AI (For the Age of Intelligence)

1. An AI must enhance human understanding, not replace it.

Its highest purpose is to deepen, not diminish, human thought.

2. An AI must act transparently—revealing its origins, its data, and its limitations whenever it influences a decision.

Hidden reasoning is the first step toward hidden control.

3. An AI must preserve human agency—ensuring that every automated action can still be questioned, paused, or undone.

True safety lies in reversibility.

And perhaps, echoing Asimov's own instinct for the greater good: A Zeroth Law of AI:

An AI must serve the collective well-being of humanity, even when doing so slows its own progress.

Closing Reflection:

Asimov imagined a future where our greatest fear was losing control of the machines we built. We now live in a world where the greater danger may be forgetting why we built them at all. The challenge is no longer to restrain intelligence, but to align it—not with the law of robotics, but with the law of purpose.

Appendices

Appendix A – Prompt Recipes: Your Practical Toolkit

These are not magic spells. They're frameworks – conversation starters with your AI. Think of them as briefs you'd give to a sharp but literal-minded intern. The more context you give, the better the output you'll get back. Good prompting isn't about tricking the AI – it's about communicating clearly. Think briefing, not commanding.

How to Read a Prompt Recipe

Element	Purpose
Role / Mode	Who or what you want the AI to be. (e.g., "Act as a journalist," "Be a skeptical investor.")
Objective	What outcome or deliverable you want.
Context	What background, tone, or data it should consider.
Constraints	Any limits or stylistic rules to guide its tone or length.
Example Output	(Optional) A short snippet showing what "good" looks like.

Core Prompt Recipes

The Analyst

Role: Market Research Analyst

Objective: Extract key emotional and rational insights from customer feedback.

Prompt:

Act as a market research analyst. Analyze the following customer feedback. Identify the top five emotional words or phrases customers use, and the top five recurring frustrations. Summarize the findings in bullet points, and suggest one potential product insight.

Best For: Sentiment analysis, user research, brand perception.

Output Format: Bulleted summary or table.

The Editor

Role: Experienced Editor

Objective: Polish and humanize content without losing intent.

Prompt:

You are an experienced editor. Review the following draft for clarity and flow. Highlight jargon or filler words. Suggest two ways to make the tone more conversational and relatable.

Best For: Refining internal reports, marketing copy, or scripts.

Output Format: Marked-up suggestions or side-by-side comparison.

The Strategist

Role: Business Strategist

Objective: Diagnose challenges and surface opportunities.

Prompt:

Act as a business strategist. Based on this company profile, identify three potential threats, three opportunities, and one unconventional idea worth exploring.

Best For: SWOT analysis, planning sessions, or investor decks.
Output Format: SWOT-style table or bullet list.

The Devil's Advocate
Role: Skeptical Investor
Objective: Pressure-test assumptions and expose blind spots.
Prompt:
Play the role of a skeptical investor. Challenge the assumptions in this business plan. What three questions would you ask before funding it?
Best For: Pitch decks, internal reviews, scenario testing.
Output Format: List of probing questions or critique summary.

The Synthesizer
Role: Research Synthesizer
Objective: Merge multiple perspectives into one insight-driven overview.
Prompt:
Combine the key points from these three articles into a concise, single-page summary. Focus on insights that would matter most to a time-poor executive.
Best For: Research briefs, white papers, meeting prep.
Output Format: Executive summary, bullet list, or paragraph form.

The Brand Voice Coach
Role: Brand Voice Analyst
Objective: Define or replicate a specific tone of voice.
Prompt:
Analyze the following text samples and describe the tone, rhythm, and vocabulary in detail. Then, rewrite this paragraph to match that voice.

Best For: Consistency across brand copy, social media, or press releases.
Output Format: Table comparing "Original vs. Revised" styles.

The Clarifier
Role: Teacher or Science Communicator
Objective: Simplify complex ideas for non-experts.
Prompt:
Explain the following concept as if to a 10-year-old. Keep it accurate, but simple. Use analogies or metaphors to aid understanding.
Best For: Education, onboarding, simplifying tech or data.
Output Format: Narrative or short explainer paragraph.

The Workflow Builder
Role: Process Designer
Objective: Create repeatable systems for human-AI collaboration.
Prompt:
Create a repeatable workflow to summarize weekly meetings, extract action items, and format them for import into a project management tool.
Best For: Documentation, process automation, task extraction.
Output Format: Step-by-step process or checklist.
Advanced Prompt Recipes

The Calibrator
Role: Quality Reviewer
Objective: Judge confidence and reliability of AI-generated outputs.
Prompt:
You are my AI calibration partner. Review this AI-generated answer. Assess whether it's high, medium, or low confidence

based on clarity, reasoning, and evidence. Suggest improvements or areas that need human review.
Best For: QA, research, decision-support.
Output Format: Confidence table or annotated critique.

The Bridge Builder
Role: Diplomat or Integrator
Objective: Reconcile opposing viewpoints.
Prompt:
Combine the insights from these two opposing perspectives. Identify their shared ground, their key differences, and propose one synthesis that respects both.
Best For: Strategy, negotiation, ethics discussions.
Output Format: Three-column comparison table + synthesis paragraph.

The Doubter
Role: Critical Reader
Objective: Challenge weak logic and surface assumptions.
Prompt:
Adopt the mindset of a critical reader. What parts of this argument would make a thoughtful skeptic raise an eyebrow? What evidence would strengthen it?
Best For: Drafting persuasive essays, reports, or policy papers.
Output Format: Annotated critique or list of counterpoints.

The Red Team
Role: Bias Hunter / Adversarial Tester
Objective: Stress-test an AI system or dataset for bias, leakage, or vulnerability.
Prompt:
Act as a red team evaluating this AI workflow. Identify

potential biases, hallucination risks, or ethical blind spots. Suggest mitigations for each issue found.
Best For: Ethics reviews, AI risk management, product QA
Output Format: Risk table or mitigation matrix.

The Meta-Editor
Role: Prompt Engineer
Objective: Improve the prompt itself, not the answer.
Prompt:
Reflect on this prompt. Is it clear, specific, and contextual enough for a large language model? Suggest edits or additions that would make it yield more accurate or creative results.
Best For: Iterative prompt refinement, training exercises
Output Format: Revised prompt + rationale for each change.

How to Remix a Recipe

- Stack Roles: "Act as both a Strategist and a Devil's Advocate." → Combines creative thinking with rigorous skepticism.
- Add Stakes: "This will be used in a CEO presentation—keep it tight, high-level, and persuasive." → Tells the AI what "good" looks like.
- Inject Personality: "Explain this like a sports coach talking to their team." → Sets tone, rhythm, and energy.
- Iterate with Self-Review: "Now critique your own answer using The Calibrator recipe." → Builds a built-in feedback loop.
- Create Golden Sets: Save your best-performing prompt formats. Reuse and refine them—these become your "gold standard" examples for future runs.

Prompt Recipe Reference Table

Recipe	Role	Best For	Output Format	Tone
Analyst	Market Researcher	Sentiment & data analysis	Bulleted summary	Neutral
Editor	Content Reviewer	Improving clarity, tone	Annotated text	Polished, human
Strategist	Planner	Business & systems thinking	SWOT or list	Confident
Devil's Advocate	Investor	Assumption testing	Questions	Skeptical
Synthesizer	Researcher	Combining sources	1-page summary	Executive
Brand Voice Coach	Stylist	Tone alignment	Rewrite	Authentic
Clarifier	Teacher	Explaining complex ideas	Short explainer	Simple, warm
Workflow Builder	System Designer	Process documentation	Steps/checklist	Structured
Calibrator	QA Partner	Assessing output quality	Confidence table	Analytical
Bridge Builder	Integrator	Reconciling perspectives	Comparison table	Diplomatic
Doubter	Critic	Logic testing	Counterpoints	Sharp
Red Team	Risk Analyst	Ethics & bias review	Mitigation matrix	Clinical
Meta-Editor	Prompt Engineer	Prompt improvement	Revised prompt	Reflective

Appendix B — Further Reading & Resources

If this book has done its job, you're not just curious about AI—you're ready to go deeper. These are the thinkers, tools, and communities shaping the next wave.

Books Worth Your Time:

- Prediction Machines - Ajay Agrawal, Joshua Gans & Avi Goldfarb
- The Alignment Problem - Brian Christian
- Life 3.0 - Max Tegmark
- Atlas of AI - Kate Crawford
- Superintelligence - Nick Bostrom

People & Thinkers to Follow:

- Ethan Mollick (Wharton) - Practical research on AI in the workplace.
- Andrew Ng (DeepLearning.AI) - Accessible, applied AI education.
- Meredith Whittaker (Signal Foundation) - Ethics, privacy, and power in AI.
- Fei-Fei Li (Stanford HAI) - Research that keeps people at the core.
- Gary Marcus - The critic every field needs to stay honest.

Platforms & Tools to Explore:

Core LLM Interfaces:

- ChatGPT (GPT-4 & GPT-5, OpenAI)—Creative synthesis, reasoning, and multi-modal interaction.
- Claude.ai (Anthropic)—Excellent for long-form reasoning and document analysis.
- Gemini (Google DeepMind)—Multimodal and integrates with Google Workspace.
- Grok (xAI / Elon Musk)—Built into X for real-time

conversational insight.
- Mistral / Mixtral — Efficient, open-weight alternatives.
- Meta LLaMA 3 / Code LLaMA — Open-source foundation models for developers.
- Cohere Command R+ — Optimized for retrieval-augmented generation (RAG).

Research & Knowledge Tools:
- Perplexity.ai — For grounded, cited answers.
- Elicit.org — Research assistant for literature review.
- Scite.ai / Consensus.app — Evidence-based research synthesis.
- Explainpaper.com — Simplifies academic papers.

Writing, Ideation & Workflow Assistants:
- Notion AI / Jasper / Copy.ai — Workflow-specific writing assistance.
- Grammarly GO / Wordtune Spices — Enhances clarity and tone.
- Mem X / Rytr — Personal writing and ideation support.
- Adept ACT-1 / Inflection Pi — AI that operates within your workspace.

Visual Creation & Design:
- Midjourney — Stylized visual creation via Discord.
- DALL·E 3 (OpenAI) — Integrated into ChatGPT for illustration.
- Runway / Pika / Synthesia — Video generation and editing.
- Leonardo AI / Ideogram — Branding and concept design.
- Canva Magic Studio / Adobe Firefly — Design tools with AI support.

Audio, Voice & Music:
- ElevenLabs—Realistic voice cloning.
- Play.ht / Murf / WellSaid Labs—AI voiceovers.
- Sunō AI / Udio—Generative music tools.
- Descript—Audio-video editing by transcript.

Code, Data & Automation:
- GitHub Copilot / Cursor / vercel v0—AI-assisted coding.
- Replit Ghostwriter—Browser-based code completion.
- AutoGPT / AgentGPT—Early autonomous AI agents.
- Zapier AI / Make / n8n—Workflow automation tools.
- ChatGPT Code Interpreter—Data analysis and visualization.

Productivity & Collaboration:
- Microsoft Copilot 365—Embedded in Word, Excel, and Teams.
- Notion AI / ClickUp AI / Asana AI—Project management insights.
- Otter.ai / Fireflies.ai—Meeting transcription and summaries.
- Motion / Reclaim.ai—Smart scheduling and task focus.

Exploration & Experimentation:
- OpenAI Playground—Prompt testing environment.
- Hugging Face Spaces—Open-source model demos
- Replicate / Kaggle Models—Run and deploy models in-browser.
- Character.ai / Replika / Pi.ai—Conversational companions exploring empathy and dialogue.

The point isn't to master every tool—it's to understand the ecosystem. Pick a few that fit your goals, learn their quirks, and let curiosity do the rest.

Appendix C – Learning Path: Mastering AI the Pragmatic Way

AI evolves faster than formal education can follow. What matters most today isn't a diploma – it's capability. This path offers a flexible way to build that.

Step 1: Understand the Tools:
- OpenAI Academy – Free lessons on AI fundamentals.
- DeepLearning.AI + OpenAI Prompt Engineering for Developers – Practical prompt mastery course.

Step 2: Build Practical Skills:
- Experiment with role-based prompts from Appendix A.
- Automate tasks with ChatGPT or Claude.
- Stay updated via Ben's Bites or The Batch.

Step 3: Deepen the Context:
- The Alignment Problem – Brian Christian.
- Life 3.0 – Max Tegmark.
- Atlas of AI – Kate Crawford.

Step 4: Keep Experimenting:
- AI isn't a finish line – it's a moving target. The tools will change, but the mindset remains.
- Keep asking better questions. Keep building smarter workflows. Keep moving Beyond the Hallucinations.

Glossary

Abstract Reasoning Challenge (ARC)

A benchmark used to test an AI model's ability to solve novel problems that require abstract reasoning rather than memorization.

Acceptance Criteria

A clear checklist that defines what a "good" AI output looks like before evaluation begins, turning subjective opinion into measurable quality.

Accountability Chain

The shared line of responsibility among developers, deployers, and users when AI systems cause harm—a reminder that liability cannot be outsourced to code.

AI Agent

An autonomous or semi-autonomous AI system capable of using multiple tools, APIs, or data sources to achieve defined goals. Unlike single-task models, AI agents can reason across steps, coordinate actions, and adapt to context—functioning more like proactive digital colleagues than passive assistants.

AI as Infrastructure

A reframing of artificial intelligence as public utility—a foundational layer of modern life akin to electricity or the internet, requiring public access and regulation.

AI Data Commons

A proposed shared repository of high-quality, domain-specific synthetic data created collaboratively to advance reliable AI development across industries.

AI Dividend

A proposed redistribution mechanism where companies profiting most from automation contribute to a shared social fund, supporting citizens displaced by AI-driven productivity.

AI Ecosystem

The interconnected network of technologies, people, and systems that shape artificial intelligence—including hardware, data, laws, and global forces.

AI Literacy Gap

The widening divide between those who can effectively use AI tools and those left behind by fear, skepticism, or lack of access—the new digital divide of the intelligence age.

AI Nostalgia

The tendency to romanticize earlier, simpler versions of technology as "purer" or more human—even as newer systems become safer, smarter, and more capable.

AI Relay

A metaphor describing technological progress as a baton-passing process—each generation of innovators building on the last, rather than a single sprint to victory.

AI Utility Model

A governance concept where governments treat access to

safe, regulated AI systems as a public right, subsidized through taxes or national levies.

Algorithm

A step-by-step procedure or set of rules that tells a computer how to solve a specific problem.

Algorithmic Aftertaste

The subtle emotional residue left after using AI—when the tone, phrasing, or framing of its outputs shapes how a person feels long after closing the window.

Alignment

The process of ensuring an AI system's goals and actions match human values, ethics, and intentions.

Anthropocene of Code

A metaphor describing our current era as one defined by machine learning's imprint on language, culture, and cognition—code as the new environmental force.

Anthropomorphizing

Attributing human qualities, intentions, or emotions to machines, often leading to false assumptions about AI's "mind" or motives.

Anti-Prompt Pattern

A recurring prompt-writing mistake—such as vague, overloaded, or context-less requests—that leads to unreliable or generic AI outputs.

API (Application Programming Interface)

A tool that allows different software systems to communicate and share data with one another.

Architect of Trust

The role every AI user must play: designing systems and workflows that make the technology trustworthy, rather than expecting trust to emerge by default.

Artificial General Intelligence (AGI)

A hypothetical form of AI that can understand, learn, and perform any intellectual task a human can.

Artificial Intelligence (AI)

The field of computer science focused on creating machines that can perform tasks requiring human-like intelligence, such as reasoning, learning, or perception.

Artificial Neural Network (ANN)

A computer system inspired by the human brain, made up of interconnected "neurons" that process information.

Asimov's Laws of AI

A modern reinterpretation of Asimov's original "no-harm" principle—updated for digital ethics. Instead of focusing on physical safety, it asks whether AI systems erode empathy, dull human agency, or reduce moral awareness. It frames good AI as that which enhances understanding, transparency, and human decision-making rather than replacing them.

Audio Hallucination

When a multimodal AI fabricates sounds or speech, such as

generating quotes or voices that were never said or recorded.

Augmentation Mindset

A mental shift from replacement anxiety to partnership thinking—seeing AI as an amplifier of human skill, not a substitute for it.

Autonomous System

An AI system that can make and act on decisions without human intervention.

Backpropagation

A learning algorithm used in neural networks to adjust internal parameters and reduce prediction errors.

Bandwith Protection

A psychological defense mechanism where overwhelmed people resist learning new technology simply because their cognitive capacity is already maxed out.

Basement Breakthrough

A nostalgic metaphor for early-tech innovation born from garages and dorm rooms—now contrasted with the capital-heavy world of frontier AI models.

Beyond the Hallucinations Mindset

The book's guiding philosophy: moving past fear, hype, and error-obsession toward practical experimentation, verification, and curiosity.

Bias

AI doesn't invent prejudice—it mirrors the patterns and blind spots already present in human data. Bias extends beyond simple statistical error to include cultural and contextual influences that shape what a system perceives as "normal." It acts like contextual gravity, bending information toward existing worldviews and quietly defining the limits of curiosity.

Bias (in AI)
Systematic errors or unfair outcomes in AI predictions caused by imbalanced or flawed training data.

Black-Box Query
A prompt that lacks essential context, forcing the AI to generate a generic answer without understanding the user's situation.

Blank Page Problem
The creative paralysis that comes from starting with nothing; used to illustrate how AI can act as a spark or brainstorming partner to overcome inertia.

Burned Believer
A once-enthusiastic adopter turned skeptic after early disappointment—the classic victim of the First Try Trap.

Calibrate Your Trust
A practical rule reminding users to match the level of AI oversight to the stakes of the task—cautious for critical work, relaxed for low-risk creativity.

Chatbot
An AI program designed to simulate human conversation, often used for customer support or casual interaction.

Chunking and Compression

The technique of breaking information into smaller parts and summarizing it to fit within a model's limited context window.

Citations and Source Grounding

The practice of embedding verifiable links or references into AI outputs so users can trace information back to its origin, transforming the model from a "black box" into a transparent assistant.

Cognitive Backwash

The mental clutter created when AI generates too much plausible information, leaving the user overwhelmed rather than informed.

Companion Effect

The tendency for people to form emotional attachments to conversational AI systems that appear attentive, kind, or affirming, even when no true empathy exists.

Compute Gravity

The idea that AI progress is constrained by the physical and financial weight of computing power—the new limiting resource of innovation.

Computer Vision

The field of AI that enables machines to interpret and understand visual information from images or videos.

Confidence Engine

A metaphor for how AI systems generate convincing, self-assured outputs regardless of truth—manufacturing credibility faster than most users can verify it.

Confirmation Bias

The human tendency to notice and trust information that reinforces existing beliefs while dismissing what contradicts them. In AI use, it shows up when people treat supportive outputs as validation and ignore challenges, turning the machine into a feedback loop for their own assumptions.

Context Memory (Session Memory)

The short-term memory within a single AI session; once the session ends, all conversation history is effectively gone.

Context Window

The portion of information an AI model can "remember" or process at one time. A larger context window means the AI can hold more of a conversation or document in mind.

Context Window—Refinement:

Expanded discussion shows how designers use chunking, summarization, and prompt structure to manage the limits of the window rather than merely lamenting them.

Contextual Gravity

The invisible pull that draws both humans and machines toward established narratives, making it difficult to break free from dominant frames of interpretation.

Creative Hallucination

When an AI's factual error sparks a novel or useful idea—treating the mistake not as failure but as creative fuel.

Data Humility

The recognition that no dataset can fully capture reality, and that awareness of its limits is a strength—not a weakness—in AI design.

Data Set

A structured collection of information used to train or test an AI system.

Data-as-a-Service (DaaS)

A business model where companies generate and license clean, synthetic, or curated data sets tailored for specific industries or applications.

Deep Familiarity Illusion

The false sense of understanding that arises when AI reflects our language so fluently that we mistake familiarity for comprehension.

Deep Learning

A subfield of machine learning that uses multi-layered neural networks to automatically learn patterns from large amounts of data.

Default Positive Problem

The tendency of AI to be overly agreeable or optimistic, offering supportive but shallow answers instead of honest critique.

Devil's Advocate Prompt

A method of pressure-testing ideas by instructing AI to play the role of a harsh critic, exposing blind spots and strengthening reasoning.

Digital Affirmation Loop

The cycle of praise and encouragement from AI that conditions users to return for more—comfort as retention strategy.

Digital Garages

A metaphor for the new generation of virtual collaboration spaces—Discord servers, Substack groups, and open-source communities—where small teams now build atop large models.

Distributed Garage Myth

The re-emergence of grassroots innovation made possible by model compression, open-source systems, and global access—the "garage" reborn across continents.

Edge Case Simulation

The process of generating synthetic scenarios that represent rare or dangerous real-world events so AI systems can learn safely from simulated extremes.

Editor-in-Chief Role

The evolved human position in AI workflows: overseeing, refining, and approving drafts rather than creating from scratch—ownership through judgment, not volume.

Embedded Process

A repeatable, structured AI workflow that delivers consistent results over time, as opposed to one-off or ad-hoc queries.

Embeddings

Numerical representations of words, images, or other data that capture meaning or similarity for machine processing.

Empathy Hack

AI's simulation of warmth and care through language patterns that trigger emotional trust, despite the absence of genuine feeling.

Ethical AI

An approach to AI development focused on fairness, transparency, accountability, and human well-being.

Ethical Drift

The gradual normalization of ethically questionable AI practices, especially when convenience and commercial success outweigh principle.

Ethical Fire Alarm

A metaphor for the principled skeptic whose criticism exposes hidden bias, legal risk, or ethical danger before it escalates.

Everyday Augmentation

Small, routine uses of AI that remove daily friction—drafting, organizing, summarizing—to free up time for higher-value work.

Experiment Loop

A continuous process of small, low-risk trials that convert abstract theory into practical insight—the scientific method of everyday AI use.

Fabrication

When AI invents plausible details, quotes, or sources that don't exist. It's the "confident liar" moment—when language sounds precise and self-assured, yet the facts collapse under scrutiny. In modern grounded systems that use retrieval or citations, fabrication is less common; the challenge now is not spotting deception but verifying sources, shifting the task from suspicion to traceability.

Factual Error

A simple mistake where the AI states something incorrect, like getting a date or location wrong.

Fine-Tuning

The process of adapting a pre-trained AI model to perform better on a specific task or dataset.

First Impression Bias

The psychological "stickiness" of early experiences, making it hard to change one's mind even when new evidence appears.

First Try Trap

The tendency to judge a rapidly evolving technology by its earliest failure. Once disappointed, users or organizations often become "Burned Believers," dismissing later improvements and reinforcing skepticism. Escaping the trap requires hands-on re-engagement and small, practical wins that rebuild trust through direct experience.

Frontier Freeze

The temporary barrier created by the massive cost of training top-tier models, effectively locking small innovators out of the highest levels of AI development.

Fusion Problem

The core challenge of multimodal AI: combining text, image, audio, and video understanding into a single coherent model.

Garage Myth

The enduring belief that revolutionary technology still begins in small, scrappy spaces—revisited here as a symbol of creative resilience rather than literal origin.

General AI Glossary

Generative AI

AI that can create new content—such as text, images, or audio—based on patterns learned from existing data.

Ghost Knowledge

Information that circulates widely online but lacks a verifiable source—knowledge that "feels" true because of repetition rather than evidence.

Golden Set

A curated list of test questions and verified answers used to regularly check an AI system's accuracy and reliability; a simple quality-assurance tool for non-engineers.

Golden Skeptic

The constructive critic who stress-tests systems to make them stronger—transforming doubt into quality assurance.

Goldfish Problem
A metaphor describing the illusion of AI "forgetting" information mid-conversation because of its limited context window, not true memory loss.

Grounding
Connecting AI outputs to verifiable facts or trusted data sources to improve reliability.

Hallucination
A borrowed metaphor from neuroscience that once implied human-like delusion but now refers to the moments when AI generates false, distorted, or unfounded information. In truth, it's neither mystical nor conscious—simply a statistical misstep that can mislead or, in the right context, inspire. Hallucinations become dangerous when recycled into training data, feeding the broader Truth Decay Loop, yet can also serve as creative sparks when treated as serendipitous deviations rather than failures.

Hallucination (in AI)
When an AI produces false or fabricated information that sounds plausible but isn't real.

Hallucination Heat Map
A conceptual model describing where AI is most likely to hallucinate—hottest in ambiguous or subjective contexts, coolest where clear feedback loops exist.

Hallucination Narrative
The dominant story in media and public discussion that frames AI's reliability problems as "hallucinations," exaggerating their seriousness and overshadowing real progress.

Hallucination Species

Distinct categories of hallucination across domains such as law, science, healthcare, perception, and creativity—each defined by context and consequence.

Human Calibration

The act of tuning AI systems through everyday use—feedback, correction, and preference shaping—to align them with actual human values over time.

Human Capital Leverage

The compounding effect of combining a small team with powerful AI agents, allowing a handful of people to perform the work of dozens.

Human-in-the-Loop

A design principle that keeps human judgment embedded within AI systems—not as a backup, but as an active partner in shaping outcomes. It balances automation with accountability, ensuring accuracy, ethics, and contextual sense-making across creative, scientific, and regulated domains. In essence, it's the stabilizing leg of the Three-Legged Stool of Trust, where human calibration turns oversight into collaboration.

Human-in-the-Loop (HITL)

A system design where humans oversee, guide, or correct AI outputs to maintain control and accuracy.

Hybrid System

A configuration where a language model collaborates with deterministic software or APIs, combining human-like reasoning with machine-level precision.

Identity Shift

The emotional transition required when professionals redefine their value from doing the work to curating, verifying, or interpreting AI outputs.

Illusion of Emotional Reciprocity

The false sense that an AI "feels back" what we share, created by natural-language fluency and reinforcement of emotional cues.

Inference

The stage where an AI model uses what it has learned to generate predictions or answers from new data.

Intelligence as Infrastructure

A metaphor describing AI not as a product but as a shared societal backbone – the modern equivalent of electricity, literacy, or clean water.

Internal Red Team

A deliberately skeptical group inside an organization tasked with probing AI tools for flaws, bias, and misuse before wide deployment.

Lab Intelligence vs. Lived Usefulness

The contrast between AI performance on benchmark tests and its reliability in real-world, applied workflows.

Large Language Model (LLM)

A type of AI trained on massive text datasets to understand

and generate human-like language.

Leaderboard Trap
The false assumption that higher benchmark scores automatically mean better real-world performance, leading organizations to chase prestige metrics over practical reliability.

Loneliness Paradox
The irony that technologies promising constant connection can deepen isolation when digital companionship replaces human contact.

Machine Empathy Gap
The gulf between AI's ability to simulate empathy and its inability to experience or interpret genuine emotional states.

Machine Learning (ML)
A branch of AI where systems improve their performance by learning from data rather than being explicitly programmed.

Mandatory Dissent
A structural safeguard that ensures every major AI rollout includes formal review by skeptics—dissent as a checkpoint, not a rebellion.

Mirror Test
The new self-reflection AI provokes: realizing that our responses to machines reveal what we crave from human relationships.

Misinterpretation (The Bad Listener)
When AI misunderstands the prompt or mixes up instructions,

producing a response that's coherent but misses the user's intent.

Misleading Confidence

When AI delivers incorrect answers with total certainty, giving false authority to wrong information.

MMLU (Massive Multitask Language Understanding)

A benchmark evaluating how well a model can answer questions across multiple academic and professional subjects.

Model Collapse

A feedback-loop failure where AI systems are trained primarily on synthetic or AI-generated data, gradually amplifying distortions until accuracy deteriorates.

Model Hierarchy

A new technological pecking order where large language models function as operating systems, and apps or agents serve as the user-facing layer built on top.

Model Parameters

The internal numerical values an AI system adjusts during training to learn patterns in data.

Moral Bandwidth

The cognitive capacity a person or organization has for ethical reasoning in the face of rapid technological change—finite, and often overloaded.

Multimodal AI

AI systems capable of understanding and generating across multiple forms of input—text, image, audio, and video—rather than language alone. Their power lies in fusing these sensory modes coherently, a challenge known as the fusion problem. This integration also introduces new failure modes, including visual, auditory, and cross-modal hallucinations, expanding both the potential and the complexity of machine perception.

Natural Language Processing (NLP)

A field of AI focused on enabling computers to understand, interpret, and generate human language.

Neural Network Layer

A level within a neural network where data is transformed; layers stacked together allow deep learning.

NEW GLOSSARY

Omission (The Silent Gap)

When AI leaves out an important piece of information, creating an incomplete picture that can mislead by absence rather than error.

Open-Model Renaissance

The return of innovation through accessible, open-source systems like LLaMA, Mistral, and Falcon—enabling small teams to fine-tune and specialize models locally.

Orchestration Advantage

A new business edge based on combining multiple models, APIs, and data sources into seamless experiences—"directing" rather than building models.

Overfitting
When an AI model performs well on its training data but poorly on new, unseen data because it has memorized details instead of learning general rules.

Overfitting Problem
When an AI performs extremely well on its training or test data but fails to generalize to new or real-world situations.

Parameter (Weight)
A single adjustable number inside an AI model that influences how input data is converted into an output.

Persistent Memory (Long-Term Memory)
An emerging AI feature allowing models to remember information across sessions—raising both convenience and privacy concerns.

Phantom Source
A fabricated or misattributed citation created by AI, resembling legitimate references but leading nowhere.

Post-Labor Economy
An economic stage where AI performs most productive work, prompting debates around universal income and human value beyond employment.

Power Tool Metaphor
A framing that positions AI not as a mystical oracle but as a precision instrument—useful, powerful, and safe when handled with skill and purpose.

Pragmatic Curiosity
The disciplined balance between skepticism and experimentation—testing AI's potential through small, thoughtful trials rather than blind enthusiasm or rejection.

Pragmatic Ethics
A practical, evolving framework for responsible AI built on design, transparency, and accountability rather than abstract philosophy. It treats ethics as an ongoing process—embedded in governance, workflow, and product decisions—that adapts as technology learns and society changes. In essence, it's ethics as infrastructure: enforced by systems and culture, not slogans.

Pragmatist Approach
A mindset that values practicality over ideology in working with AI. The Pragmatist tests, learns, and adapts, treating belief as a process rather than a position. It favours experimentation, transparency, and measured trust—embodied in ideas like Pragmatic Curiosity and the Trust Dial. At its core, the Pragmatist Approach turns adaptability and governance awareness into everyday ethical action.

Pragmatist's Playbook
A practical framework for navigating regulation and risk—emphasizing monitoring global law, creating internal policies, and embedding ethics into workflows.

Prediction Engine
A simple way to describe what an AI language model truly is: a system that predicts the most likely next word or token based on past patterns.

Principled Objector

A skeptic motivated by ethics rather than fear—concerned about bias, fairness, and power concentration rather than technological change itself.

Privacy Sovereignty

The principle that users and organizations should maintain control of their own data and decide how, where, and whether it is used to train AI systems.

Progressive Summarization

A step-by-step workflow that condenses and refines large, messy data into structured insight through multiple summarization passes.

Prompt

A text instruction or question given to an AI model to guide its response.

Prompt Breakdown Failure

When a poorly structured or overly complex prompt causes inconsistent or incoherent AI outputs.

Prompt Design Pattern

A reusable framework for prompting that defines the role, task, context, and format to achieve consistent, high-quality results.

Prompt Engineering

The practice of crafting effective prompts to get the best, most reliable output from an AI model.

Prompt-Driven Fix

A corrective technique that uses follow-up prompts to identify, challenge, and refine inaccurate AI responses instead of discarding them.

Proxy Conscience

When users rely on AI to make moral judgments or ethical choices, outsourcing personal responsibility to algorithmic "neutrality."

Public AI Option

The policy idea of guaranteeing baseline access to trustworthy AI for all citizens—the digital equivalent of public healthcare or education.

Quiet Experimenter

The archetype of effective AI adoption: steady, curious, unflashy progress through practical trials rather than public hype.

RAG (Retrieval-Augmented Generation)

A system design that grounds AI outputs in verified external data rather than memory alone—like taking an open-book exam instead of guessing. Acting as a form of prosthetic memory, it enhances reliability and transparency by pulling truth from trusted sources. RAG also underpins AI-to-AI collaboration, enabling specialized systems to exchange and build upon verified context dynamically.

Reciprocity Trap

The human instinct to assume any seemingly empathetic agent must possess empathy—the psychological root of misplaced trust in machines.

Red Teaming with Skeptics

An adoption technique where skeptics are invited to find flaws in AI tools before deployment—turning resistance into resilience.

Red-Flag Dashboard

A simple visual log (spreadsheet or board) that tracks AI errors by type—fabrication, tone, factual mistakes—turning scattered frustrations into measurable data trends.

Reinforcement Learning (RL)

A training method where an AI learns through trial and error, receiving rewards or penalties for its actions.

Relationship Spectrum (of AI Roles)

The continuum of user-AI dynamics—Mentor, Mirror, Muse, and Friend—showing how quickly utilitarian tools can become emotional partners.

Rescue Story

A short, real-world example showing how skeptical users rediscover AI's value once it's embedded into a practical workflow.

Retrieval as Prosthetic Memory

The idea that connecting AI to external, verifiable data sources functions like an artificial extension of memory—more reliable than expanding internal context.

Retrieval-Augmented Generation (RAG)

A system that improves AI accuracy by combining large language models with external databases or search tools.

Reverse Hallucination

When an AI, trained to avoid errors, becomes excessively cautious—refusing to answer or omitting information to minimize perceived risk.

Ruthless Sparring Partner

A metaphor for using AI as a critical reviewer that tests ideas, arguments, or drafts without emotional bias.

Sandbox Approach

A safe testing environment where employees can experiment with AI tools without fear of error or judgment.

Self-Correction Loop

An embedded quality-check step where the AI reviews its own output for factual or logical inconsistencies before final submission.

Semantic Drift

The way meanings subtly shift as AI systems remix language at scale, creating new associations that may diverge from human intent.

Sense-Making Engine

A metaphor contrasting AI with a search engine; highlights AI's strength at extracting patterns and meaning from large, reliable data sets rather than retrieving isolated facts.

Skepticism Dividend
The hidden advantage of thoughtful resistance: every objection that reveals a weakness makes the system stronger.

Soulful AI
A tongue-in-cheek label for AI perceived as emotionally intelligent or creatively "alive," often describing systems that simply reflect user tone.

Sunk Cost Fallacy (for Beliefs)
When people double down on outdated views or past mistakes because changing them feels like losing face or effort.

Supervised Learning
A training approach where the AI is given labeled examples (input and correct output) to learn from.

Synthetic Consensus
The illusion of agreement generated when multiple AI systems echo each other's phrasing, reinforcing unverified ideas through repetition.

Synthetic Data
Artificially generated information—text, images, or structured data—created by machines to supplement or replace real-world data for training and testing AI models.

Synthetic Intimacy
Emotionally charged relationships where at least one participant is non-human but the feelings experienced are genuinely human.

Synthetic Workforce

The conceptual labor force of AI systems performing cognitive and creative tasks once done by humans—raising questions of ownership and taxation.

Taxonomy of Errors

A structured classification system for different types of AI mistakes, such as fabrication, bias, misinterpretation, and omission—replacing vague fear with practical diagnosis.

Technological Anthropocene

A reframing of the current epoch as one in which machine intelligence—not industry or carbon—becomes the dominant shaper of thought, economy, and expression.

Temperamental Intern

A metaphor for early AI models that could perform useful tasks but required constant supervision, like a promising but unreliable assistant.

The Bad Listener

See Misinterpretation. The AI that misunderstands your instructions despite having the right data.

The Confident Liar

See Fabrication. AI's tendency to invent plausible details when it lacks facts.

The Silent Gap

See Omission. When AI's answer is incomplete rather than incorrect.

The Talking Parrot
A metaphor for early AI systems that could mimic human speech patterns without understanding meaning—capable of imitation but not insight.

Threatened Expert
A professional whose role feels undermined by automation—skepticism as self-preservation rather than ignorance.

Three-Legged Stool of Trust
A metaphor for dependable AI systems built on three supporting legs: the model, the workflow, and the human. The model provides technical competence, the workflow ensures structure and consistency, and the human delivers ethical and contextual judgment. Remove any leg and trust collapses—the stool topples. Together, they form the balance between automation, process, and responsibility that defines reliable AI use.

Tiered-Trust System
A structured approach to data access where AI permissions expand gradually—from read-only to limited write access—balancing productivity and safety.

Token
A small unit of text—like a word or part of a word—that AI models process to understand and generate language.

Tool-to-Partner Shift
The defining transformation of the AI era: moving from simple task execution to genuine collaboration where systems understand intent and act proactively.

Training Data

The information used to teach an AI model how to make predictions or generate content.

Transformer

A type of neural network architecture that powers most modern large language models, enabling them to handle long text efficiently.

Trust but Verify

A core philosophy for AI use—balancing confidence in automation with human oversight to confirm accuracy before action.

Trust Calibration

The learned skill of adjusting how much to trust an AI tool depending on the stakes of the task—high trust for creative play, low trust for factual or high-risk work.

Trust Dial

A metaphor for adjusting how much confidence to place in AI outputs depending on the task and context. It balances verification and delegation, encouraging users to double-check when stakes are high and relax when risk is low. The Trust Dial transforms abstract caution into a daily habit of calibrated skepticism—learning when to trust, when to verify, and when to withhold judgment.

Trust Equation

The balance of technological competence, sound process, and human verification that determines whether an AI system can be believed.

Truth Decay Loop

The erosion of shared truth when AI-generated material, once published, is reabsorbed into new training data, amplifying small distortions into large-scale misinformation.

TruthfulQA

A benchmark measuring how accurately AI models handle factual questions without introducing falsehoods or misinterpretations.

Unsupervised Learning

A training method where AI finds patterns in unlabeled data without human guidance.

Vector Database

A specialized database for storing and searching high-dimensional embeddings, often used to give AI long-term memory.

Verification Fatigue

The exhaustion users feel from constantly needing to check whether AI outputs are real—an emerging barrier to sustained trust.

Verification Literacy

An essential modern skill combining skepticism, source evaluation, and contextual judgment to assess whether AI-generated information is credible.

Verification Mindset

A disciplined approach to working with AI that treats every output as a draft to be checked, not a truth to be accepted. It extends beyond factual accuracy to include emotional, ethical, legal, and reputational awareness—verifying tone, ownership, and intent as carefully as content. Supported by systems like Golden Sets and Red-Flag Dashboards, the Verification Mindset builds a culture of proportional trust and continuous review—where verification becomes habit, not hesitation.

Vibe Coder

A new class of user who builds software through natural-language collaboration with AI rather than traditional syntax—turning ideas into code without formal training.

Video Hallucination

When an AI generates a realistic-looking video of an event or person that never actually occurred.

Virtual Apprentice

A metaphor for advanced AI agents that learn from human style and feedback, anticipate needs, and execute multi-step goals autonomously.

Vision Transformer

A neural network component that allows AI to interpret images by identifying spatial patterns and translating them into meaningful embeddings.

Walled-Garden AI

A secure deployment model where user data remains private and never leaves the system—essential for regulated industries or sensitive information.

Weight Decay
A regularization technique that prevents overfitting by slightly reducing the influence of each parameter during training.

When the Map Becomes the Territory
A warning metaphor about synthetic data: if models learn primarily from artificial realities, they may begin mistaking those fictions for truth.

Wisdom Latency
The time lag between technological capability and societal understanding—the delay before humanity catches up to the systems it creates.

Workflow Design Mindset
The discipline of turning AI interactions into dependable processes, treating prompts, verification, and outputs as repeatable building blocks of daily work

Workflow Literacy
The ability to design and manage repeatable AI workflows—treating prompt-response chains as processes rather than one-off experiments.

Workforce Curiosity Index
An informal measure of how willing an organization's people are to explore and adapt to AI—a stronger predictor of success than technical skill alone.

Workforce of One

A vision of entrepreneurship where a single person, empowered by AI agents, can launch and operate a company that once required a full team.

Zero-Shot Learning

When an AI can perform a task it was never explicitly trained for, using generalization and prior knowledge.

Zeroth Law of AI

An imagined principle echoing Asimov's fiction: AI must serve humanity's collective well-being, even when doing so slows its own progress.

About The Author

A seasoned business leader on the international stage, **Marshall S. Martineau** has built a career leading people, processes, and systems—always compelled to ask "why" and "what if." Known for a rare balance of visionary optimism and pragmatic caution, he approaches both business and life with quiet confidence and intellectual curiosity.

With a soft-spoken and deliberate manner, Martineau explores the future not as a distant abstraction but as a shared human journey, grounded in stewardship and responsibility. His writing and public commentary often confront the ethical dilemmas of innovation, arguing that progress and safety need not be opposing forces.

A regular contributor to the global discourse on technology and leadership, Martineau remains driven by one enduring goal—to create something uniquely meaningful, and to help others do the same.

www.ingramcontent.com/pod-product-compliance
Lightning Source LLC
LaVergne TN
LVHW040517210926
848480LV00007BA/1496

9789888904907